Contents

Chapter 3
Fraud and Abuse Waivers 59

Chapter 4
Sources of Guidance 65

Chapter 5
Related Statutes 79

About the Authors

Authors .d edition of *What Is . . . The Anti-Kickback Statute?*

Samantha Kingsbury is Of Counsel in Mintz's Health Law Practice, based in the Boston office. Samantha's practice focuses on health care enforcement defense matters, which often involve criminal, civil, and/or administrative actions brought against health care providers and companies by state and federal governmental and regulatory agencies, including the U.S. Department of Justice and the offices of its U.S. attorneys. She advises clients on issues related to the Anti-Kickback Statute, the Stark Law, the False Claims Act, and the Eliminating Kickbacks in Recovery Act, as well as state statutes prohibiting kickbacks, self-referrals, and the submission of false claims. Samantha also assists clients with conducting internal investigations, preparing self-disclosures to relevant agencies and/or payors, and developing internal compliance programs.

Karen Lovitch is the chair of Mintz's Health Law and Health Care Enforcement Defense Practices. Karen advises clients on the legal, practical, and fraud and abuse implications of business arrangements and sales and marketing practices. Her experience includes matters related to the Anti-Kickback Statute, the Stark Law, state statutes prohibiting kickbacks and self-referrals, and the federal Physician Payments Sunshine Act.

Karen applies her compliance and regulatory experience in transactional as well as litigation contexts. In addition to counseling health care entities on regulatory matters arising in connection with mergers and acquisitions, she has successfully defended clients subject to False Claims Act and other state and federal government investigations and surveys.

Rachel Yount is an associate at Mintz, based in the Washington, D.C., office. She is well versed in the federal anti-kickback statute, the Stark Law, state fraud and abuse laws, beneficiary inducement prohibitions, provider-based rules, Medicare and Medicaid program requirements, and the federal Physician Payments Sunshine Act. She routinely advises clients on the legal, practical, and fraud and abuse implications of business arrangements and sales and marketing practices. Rachel regularly assists with implementing effective health care compliance programs for clients in various health care sectors, including managed care organizations, health systems, and pharmaceutical manufacturers, to name a few. She has assisted both with developing brand new compliance programs for health care companies just starting out and maturing existing compliance programs to support health care companies' efforts to expand.

Co-authors of first edition of *What Is . . . The Anti-Kickback Statute?*

Thomas S. Crane was a member at Mintz until he retired in 2021. Before Tom's retirement, he advised national and local clients on structuring complex strategic affiliation arrangements and transactions to comply with the applicable fraud and abuse laws as well as the variety of other regulatory requirements. His work in defending clients against Anti-Kickback Statute, Stark Law, false claims, and whistleblower allegations included litigation, internal investigations, voluntary disclosures, and negotiating settlements and corporate integrity agreements. Tom was nationally recognized for his fraud and abuse experience.

Carrie Roll is a vice president and associate general counsel of Aledade, Inc., a health care IT company focused on providing independent primary care practices with the support, tools, and regulatory expertise they need to succeed in value-based care. She counsels a wide variety of business teams at Aledade on regulatory, operational, and fraud and abuse matters, including structuring proposed business arrangements to comply with the Anti-Kickback Statute, Stark Law, state anti-kickback and self-referral laws, and corporate practice of medicine and fee-splitting laws. Carrie also works on various transactions, including joint ventures, mergers and acquisitions, stock and asset purchase agreements, and service agreements. Prior to joining Aledade, Carrie was the general counsel and chief compliance officer of US Fertility, LLC where she provided legal and business advice to the largest network of infertility clinics in the United States. Carrie began her legal career as an associate at Mintz, Levin, Cohn, Ferris, Glovsky and Popeo P.C., based in the Washington, D.C., office. While there, Carrie counseled a wide range of health care providers on a variety of transactional, regulatory, and fraud and abuse matters.

Overview of the Anti-Kickback Statute and Its Purpose

1.1 Introduction

The federal Anti-Kickback Statute (AKS) is one of the best-known federal fraud and abuse statutes, due largely to its wide-ranging effects on business relationships in the health care, pharmaceutical, and medical device sectors. The AKS is a criminal statute that prohibits transactions intended to induce or reward referrals for items or services reimbursed by the federal health care programs, including Medicare, Medicaid, and TRICARE.[1] At its heart, it is an anti-corruption statute designed to protect federal health care program beneficiaries from the influence of money on referral decisions[2] and thus is intended to guard against overutilization, increased costs, and poor quality services.[3]

---

1. 42 U.S.C. § 1320a–7b(b).
2. *See* United States v. Shaw, 106 F. Supp. 2d 103, 111 (D. Mass. 2000) (citing H.R. REP. NO. 95-393, pt. 2, at 44 (1977), *reprinted in* 1977 U.S.C.C.A.N. 3039, 3047–56).
3. *See id.* at 110–11 (citing H.R. REP. NO. 92-231, 92d Cong., 1st Sess. 108 (1971), *reprinted in* 1972 U.S.C.C.A.N. 4989, 5093 (providing that the AKS was intended to prohibit "certain practices . . . [that] contributed appreciably to the cost of the Medicare and Medicaid programs")). *See generally* OIG

1.2 Statutory Language

Specifically, the AKS states as follows:

(1) Whoever *knowingly and willfully* solicits or receives *any remuneration* (including any kickback, bribe, or rebate) *directly or indirectly*, overtly or covertly, in cash or in kind—
   (A) in return for referring an individual to a person for the furnishing or arranging for the furnishing of any item or service for which payment may be made in whole or in part under a Federal health care program, or
   (B) in return for purchasing, leasing, ordering, or *arranging for or recommending* purchasing, leasing, or ordering any good, facility, service, or item for which payment may be made in whole or in part under a Federal health care program, shall be guilty of a felony and upon conviction thereof, shall be fined not more than $100,000 or imprisoned for not more than ten years, or both.
(2) Whoever knowingly and willfully offers or pays any remuneration (including any kickback, bribe, or rebate) directly or indirectly, overtly or covertly, in cash or in kind to any person *to induce* such person—
   (A) to refer an individual to a person for the furnishing or arranging for the furnishing of any item or service for which payment may be made in whole or in part under a Federal health care program, or
   (B) to purchase, lease, order, or arrange for or recommend purchasing, leasing, or ordering any good, facility, service, or item for which payment may be made in whole or in

---

Compliance Program Guidance for Pharmaceutical Manufacturers, 68 Fed. Reg. 23,731, 23,734 (May 5, 2003) (noting that, in analyzing whether their business arrangements may run afoul of the AKS, companies should ask: "Does the arrangement or practice have a potential to increase costs to the federal health care programs, beneficiaries, or enrollees? . . . Does the arrangement or practice have a potential to increase the risk of overutilization or inappropriate utilization? Does the arrangement or practice raise patient safety or quality of care concerns?").

part under a Federal health care program, shall be guilty of a felony and upon conviction thereof, shall be fined not more than $100,000 or imprisoned for not more than ten years, or both.[4]

As the text makes clear, the AKS prohibits anyone from knowingly and willfully offering, making, soliciting, or receiving any payment in return for (1) referring an individual to another person or entity for the furnishing of any item or service reimbursed by a federal health care program, or (2) recommending or arranging for the ordering of any service reimbursed by a federal health care program.[5] In other words, soliciting or accepting payments for referrals or for otherwise generating Medicare or Medicaid business is as illegal as offering or making such payments.

Because the AKS is so broad and thus can be read to encompass well-accepted and beneficial health care industry business practices, Congress included a number of exceptions and also directed the Secretary of the U.S. Department of Health and Human Services (HHS) to promulgate regulations specifying business arrangements that would be immune from enforcement activities, which are known as "safe harbors." If a business practice falls squarely within a safe harbor, it is not subject to AKS liability, but failure to comply with each element of a safe harbor does not necessarily render the activity illegal. The statutory exceptions and safe harbor regulations are discussed in more detail in Chapter 2.

---

4. 42 U.S.C. § 1320a-7b(b)(1)–(2) (emphasis added). As discussed in Section 1.3, the Bipartisan Budget Act of 2018 increased the criminal penalties under the AKS from $25,000 to $100,000 and the maximum sentence from five years to ten years. Bipartisan Budget Act of 2018, Pub. L. No. 115-123, 132 Stat. 208, 220 (2018).
5. *See id.*

1.3 Legislative and Regulatory History

Congress established the Medicare and Medicaid programs in 1965. Soon thereafter certain unethical provider practices began to develop. Physicians began profiting from the federal government by making unnecessary patient referrals (in exchange for kickbacks) to particular facilities for medical services reimbursed by the federal health care programs, which resulted in rising costs.[6] Problematic arrangements took various forms, including percentage lease agreements and payment of test interpretation fees to physicians who referred testing without performing the interpretation themselves.[7]

To combat these unethical practices, Congress passed the original version of the AKS in 1972.[8] The statute made the receipt of kickbacks, bribes, or rebates in connection with items or services covered by the Medicare and Medicaid programs a misdemeanor punishable by a fine, imprisonment, or both.[9] In 1977, Congress strengthened the AKS by, among other things, broadening the statutory language to also prohibit the offer or receipt of "any remuneration" to induce a referral, elevating the misdemeanor classification to a felony, and increasing the maximum statutory penalties.[10]

In 1980, Congress revised the AKS's intent standard to require proof that the defendant acted "knowingly and willfully" when committing acts prohibited by the statute.[11] Congress included this heightened standard out of a concern that "criminal penalties may

---

6. *See Shaw*, 106 F. Supp. 2d at 110–11; John. J. Farley, *The Medicare Antifraud Statute and Safe Harbor Regulations: Suggestions for Change*, 81 Geo. L.J. 167, 169–70 (1992).

7. *See Shaw*, 106 F. Supp. 2d at 110–11; Farley, *supra* note 6, at 169–70.

8. *See Shaw*, 106 F. Supp. 2d at 110–11.

9. *See* Farley, *supra* note 6, at 170; Social Security Amendments of 1972, Pub. L. No. 92-603, 86 Stat. 1329, 1419 (1972).

10. *See* Robert Fabrikant, Health Care Fraud Enforcement and Compliance, 3-32–3-33 (2006); *see also Shaw*, 106 F. Supp. 2d at 111 (citing H.R. Rep. No. 95-393, pt. 2, at 44 (1977), *reprinted in* 1977 U.S.C.C.A.N. 3039, 3047–56).

11. Medicare and Medicaid Amendments of 1980, Pub. L. No. 96-499, § 917, 94 Stat. 2609, 2625 (1980); *see also* Fabrikant, *supra* note 10, at 3-33.

be imposed under [then] current law to an individual whose conduct, while improper, was inadvertent."[12]

Congress next amended the AKS in 1987 when it passed the Medicare and Medicaid Patient and Program Protection Act (MMPPPA), which made two important changes to the AKS to address complaints that the 1977 amendments effectively prohibited long-standing industry practices necessary to the day-to-day operations of many providers.[13] First, the MMPPPA granted to the Office of Inspector General (OIG) the authority to exclude from participation in various federal health care programs an individual or entity convicted of an AKS violation.[14] Exclusionary authority was designed to provide a civil remedy alternative to criminal prosecution.[15] Second, the legislation directed HHS to promulgate regulations that created additional exceptions to the AKS, referred to as "safe harbors."[16] On July 29, 1991, the OIG issued the first in a series of regulations implementing the safe harbors.[17]

In 1996, Congress further amended the AKS through the Health Insurance Portability and Accountability Act (HIPAA).[18] HIPAA made three significant changes to the AKS: (1) extending its reach beyond Medicare and state health care programs to apply to services covered by the "federal health care programs";[19] (2) adding a new exception to the AKS relating to certain risk-sharing organizations;[20] and (3) enhancing communication between the OIG and the public about

---

12. Fabrikant, *supra* note 10, at 3-33 (citing H.R. Rep. No. 96-1167, 96th Cong., 2d Sess. 59 (1980), *reprinted in* 1980 U.S.C.C.A.N. 5526, 5572).
13. *See* Medicare and Medicaid Patient and Program Protection Act of 1987, Pub. L. No. 100-93, 101 Stat. 680 (1987) (codified at 42 U.S.C. § 1320a-7(b)(7)).
14. *See id.* § 2.
15. Medicare and State Health Care Programs: Fraud and Abuse; OIG Anti-Kickback, 56 Fed. Reg. 35,952 (July 29, 1991).
16. Medicare and Medicaid Patient and Program Protection Act of 1987, Pub. L. No. 100-93, § 14, 101 Stat. 680, 697–98.
17. Medicare and State Health Care Programs: Fraud and Abuse; OIG Anti-Kickback, 56 Fed. Reg. 35,952 (July 29, 1991).
18. Health Insurance Portability and Accountability Act, Pub. L. No. 104-191, 110 Stat. 1936 (Aug. 21, 1996).
19. *Id.* § 204; *see also* Fabrikant, *supra* note 10, at 3-36.
20. Health Insurance Portability and Accountability Act, § 216.

the applicability of the AKS to certain transactions.[21] Congress also directed the OIG to develop standards related to the new risk-sharing exception and to solicit proposals for new safe harbors, modifications to existing safe harbors, and fraud alerts regarding inappropriate conduct.[22] Finally, HIPAA required the OIG to establish a procedure whereby providers could request advisory opinions regarding the applicability of the AKS or a safe harbor to a given arrangement.[23]

In 1997, Congress again amended the AKS, this time adding a civil monetary penalty.[24] By adding a civil monetary penalty (and thereby lowering the burden of proof that prosecutors had to meet to impose this civil, as opposed to criminal, sanction), Congress provided prosecutors with an additional tool to combat potential fraud. The new provision established penalties of $50,000 for each act committed in violation of the AKS and damages of up to three times the amount of the prohibited remuneration.[25]

In 2010, the Patient Protection and Affordable Care Act (ACA) became law and made a number of changes to the AKS, including "expanding" its intent standard (as discussed in Section 1.4) and specifying that violations of the AKS may trigger liability under the False Claims Act (which will be discussed in more detail in Section 5.1).

Finally, in 2018, the Bipartisan Budget Act of 2018 increased the criminal fine for violating the AKS from $25,000 to $100,000, and doubled the maximum jail time for a felony conviction to ten years, bringing it in line with the maximum penalty for violating the Health Care Fraud Statute.[26]

As discussed in more detail in Section 4.1, the OIG has built upon the AKS by adopting new safe harbors and revising the original safe

---

21. *Id.* §§ 205, 216; *see also* Fabrikant, *supra* note 10, at 3-37.
22. Health Insurance Portability and Accountability Act §§ 205, 216.
23. *Id.* § 205.
24. Balanced Budget Act of 1997, Pub. L. No. 105-33, § 4304(b), 111 Stat. 251, 383–84 (1997).
25. *Id.* § 4304(b)(1)(C) (amending 42 U.S.C. § 1320a-7a(a)).
26. Bipartisan Budget Act of 2018, Pub. L. No. 115-123, 132 Stat. 208, 220 (2018); Health Care Fraud Statute, 18 U.S.C. § 1347.

harbors promulgated in 1991. This process began in 1999 when the OIG clarified the existing 1991 safe harbors and added additional safe harbors.[27] The OIG has gradually added additional safe harbors, and the total now stands at 35 safe harbors. The preambles to these rules continue to serve as valuable sources of OIG guidance on its interpretation of the AKS and the safe harbors. See Table 1 in Section 4.1 for brief descriptions of the safe harbors added in each final rule.

1.4 Key Terms

The meaning and scope of several AKS elements—including "knowingly and willfully," "remuneration," "directly or indirectly," "inducement," "arranging for or recommending," "Federal Health Care Program," and "referral"—have been the subject of considerable debate since passage of the AKS. A full understanding of these terms is essential to structuring arrangements to comply with the AKS and to avoiding enforcement challenges.

1.4.1 Knowingly and Willfully

An individual or entity must have acted "knowingly and willfully" for an AKS violation to occur. This scienter element did not appear in the original version of the statute nor in the 1977 amendments, but was added by Congress in 1980 to ensure that criminal penalties would not be imposed on those who engage in potentially improper yet inadvertent conduct.[28] Over the years, a number of courts have interpreted the AKS as requiring the government to demonstrate

---

27. *See* Federal Health Care Programs: Fraud and Abuse; Statutory Exception to the Anti-Kickback Statute for Shared Risk Arrangements, 64 Fed. Reg. 63,504 (Nov. 19, 1999); Medicare and State Health Care Programs: Fraud and Abuse; Clarification of the Initial OIG Safe Harbor Provisions and Establishment of Additional Safe Harbor Provisions under the Anti-Kickback Statute, 64 Fed. Reg. 63,518 (Nov. 19, 1999); Medicare and State Health Care Programs: Fraud and Abuse; Revisions to Safe Harbors Under the Anti-Kickback Statute, and Civil Monetary Penalty Rules Regarding Beneficiary Inducements, 85 Fed. Reg. 77,684 (Dec. 2, 2020).

28. FABRIKANT, *supra* note 10, at 3-33 (citing Omnibus Reconciliation Act of 1980, H.R. REP. No. 96-1167, 96th Cong., 2d Sess. 59, *reprinted in* 1980 U.S.C.C.A.N. 5526, 5572).

specific intent, which is a high burden of proof, but in 2010 the ACA amended the AKS to lower this standard, which made it easier for the government to prove an AKS violation.[29]

Before passage of the ACA, various judicial circuits employed different interpretations of "knowingly and willfully." For example, in *Hanlester Network v. Shalala*, a well-known case decided by the U.S. Court of Appeals for the Ninth Circuit in 1995, the court held that a party violates the AKS only if he or she (1) knew that the AKS prohibits offering or paying remuneration to induce referrals, and (2) engaged in the prohibited conduct with the specific intent to disobey the law.[30] In contrast, in *United States v. Jain*, the Eighth Circuit held that the AKS only requires proof that the defendant knew that his conduct was wrongful, as opposed to proof that he knew it violated a "known legal duty." The *Jain* court held that a good-faith belief in the legality of an arrangement was a defense to prosecution under the AKS but ultimately affirmed the defendant's conviction.[31] In *United States v. Starks*, the Eleventh Circuit found that the government need only prove that the defendant had knowledge that his or her conduct was unlawful to sustain a conviction under the AKS and thus is not required to demonstrate that the defendant knew that the conduct specifically violated the AKS.[32]

The ACA's amendment to the AKS superseded these (and all other) judicial interpretations by adding the following: "With respect to violations of the [AKS], a person need not have actual knowledge of [the AKS], or specific intent to commit a violation of [the AKS]."[33]

---

29. Patient Protection and Affordable Care Act, Pub. L. No. 111-148, § 6402(f)(2), 124 Stat. 119, 759 (2010) (codified at 18 U.S.C. § 1347(b)).
30. Hanlester Network v. Shalala, 51 F.3d 1390, 1400 (9th Cir. 1995).
31. United States v. Jain, 93 F.3d 436 (8th Cir. 1996).
32. United States v. Starks, 157 F.3d 833 (11th Cir. 1998). Still other jurisdictions have interpreted this standard differently. In *Zimmer, Inc. v. Nu Tech Medical, Inc.*, for example, the District Court for the Northern District of Indiana found that the AKS requires that defendants "knowingly and willfully" intend to engage in the prohibited acts, not that they "knowingly and willfully" intend to violate the AKS. Zimmer, Inc. v. Nu Tech Med., Inc., 54 F. Supp. 2d 850, 862 (N.D. Ind. 1999).
33. Patient Protection and Affordable Care Act, Pub. L. No. 111-148, § 6402(f), 124 Stat. 119, 759 (codified at Social Security Act § 1128B(h), 42 U.S.C. § 1320a-7b(h)).

This amendment effectively eliminated the body of case law requiring a showing of specific knowledge of and intent to violate the AKS.

1.4.2 Remuneration

The AKS prohibits the offer, receipt, payment, or solicitation of "remuneration" directly or indirectly, overtly or covertly, in cash or in kind to induce referrals. Understanding and defining "remuneration" is at the heart of any analysis under the AKS. A related and equally important concept is that of "inducement." Courts have considered whether something constitutes remuneration together with the question of whether such remuneration was offered with the intent to induce referrals.

On its face, the AKS expansively defines remuneration to include bribes, kickbacks, and rebates, whether made "directly or indirectly, overtly or covertly, in case or in kind."[34] In other words, "remuneration" is not limited to tangible items that are traditionally understood to have value (e.g., money or gifts) but may include in-kind transfers of value, such as services or discounts. For example, if a provider relieves a referral source of some obligation or burden by offering services for free, or at a price that is below fair market value, those services could constitute "remuneration" because the provider relieved the referral source of a financial obligation.

In various advisory opinions and other sources of AKS guidance, the OIG has focused its analysis on whether the item or service offered or given to a person had independent value to that person, as opposed to whether the item or service had general commercial value. This interpretation first arose in the early 1990s when the OIG responded to arguments made by the clinical laboratory industry that a laboratory could furnish a referring physician with a dedicated fax machine exclusively for transmitting test orders to the laboratory and test results back to the physician because the equipment could be used only in connection with orders submitted to and reports received from the laboratory. In the preamble to the 1991 safe har-

---

34. 42 U.S.C. § 1320a-7b(b)(1).

bor regulations, the OIG distinguished fax and other types of dedicated machines (e.g., printers) that have no value independent of the laboratory's services, and standard personal computers given to physicians that could be used for other, unrelated purposes.[35] In a 1997 letter, the OIG further clarified that the test for whether free or loaner equipment violates the AKS depends on the substance, and not the form, of the gift or loan arrangement. Merely including language in an agreement that the free or loaned multiuse equipment can only be used in connection with the services provided is insufficient to demonstrate that there is no independent value to the person receiving the loaned equipment.[36]

Other important considerations in determining whether "remuneration" offered or given to a referral source is illegal are (1) whether the value of the remuneration is above or below fair market value, and (2) the direction in which the remuneration and the potential referrals flow. A fair market value payment can still constitute illegal remuneration to induce referrals, but such a payment is typically evidence of a lawful arrangement while payments that are not fair market value may implicate the AKS. But this analysis only has meaning when viewed in the context of the flow of value. In other words, problematic arrangements arise where a provider offers or gives remuneration *to a referral source* and, in return, that referral source makes a referral to the provider for items or services reimbursable by a federal health care program. Figure 1 shows a potentially problematic arrangement.

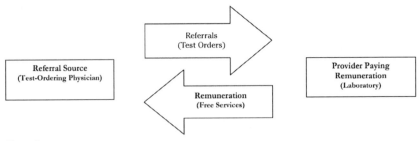

Figure 1

35. Medicare and State Health Care Programs: Fraud and Abuse; OIG Anti-Kickback, 56 Fed. Reg. at 35,978.
36. *See* OIG, Letter Re: Free Computers, Facsimile Machines and Other Goods (July 3, 1997), https://oig.hhs.gov/fraud/docs/safeharborregulations/freecomputers.htm.

Simply put, the AKS is implicated only if the remuneration flows in the opposite direction from the referrals. If a provider is overpaying a referral source for services, the implication is that the provider is doing so to induce referrals. Conversely, if a provider is underpaying a referral source for services, the provider's motive is less likely to be improper. In sum, non-fair-market-value payments are not per se unlawful, but must be analyzed closely.

A number of important cases address the issue of remuneration. For example, in *Hanlester Network*, the Ninth Circuit considered the definition of "remuneration." There, the court overturned the decisions of an administrative law judge and the Departmental Appeals Board (DAB) to exclude from participation in federal health care programs the principals involved in promoting a group of physician-owned joint venture laboratories based on their violation of the AKS. Adopting the broad definition of remuneration applied by the OIG and the DAB, the court agreed with the definition of "remuneration" previously applied in *United States v. Bay State Ambulance & Hospital Rental Service, Inc.*, where the First Circuit observed that remuneration includes "both sums for which no actual service was performed, and sums for which some service was performed."[37] As observed by the Ninth Circuit, "The phrase 'any remuneration' was intended to broaden the reach of the law which previously referred only to kickbacks, bribes, and rebates."[38]

1.4.3 Directly or Indirectly

Although the phrase "directly or indirectly" has not received much attention over the years, it is notable that Congress intentionally added these terms to the AKS to ensure that it covers the transfer of anything of value in any form or manner.[39] For example, a provider cannot evade application of the AKS by asking a third party to offer or give something of value to a referral source.

---

37. *Hanlester*, 51 F.3d at 1401 (citing United States v. Bay State Ambulance & Hosp. Rental Servs., 874 F.2d 20, 30 (1st Cir. 1989)).
38. *Id.* at 1398.
39. Medicare and State Health Care Programs: Fraud and Abuse; OIG Anti-Kickback, 56 Fed. Reg. at 35,958.

1.4.4 Inducement

The "inducement" element, which is often analyzed along with the scienter requirement (i.e., whether there was intent to induce referrals), is at the heart of every AKS analysis. As observed by the First Circuit in *Bay State*, the "gravamen of Medicare fraud is inducement."[40]

1.4.4.1   Inducement Defined

Many courts, as well as the OIG, have interpreted "inducement" in the context of the AKS to mean "to lead or move by influence or persuasion."[41] In *Hanlester*, the Ninth Circuit further explained that "inducement" means "an intent to exercise influence over the reason or judgment of another in an effort to cause the referral of program-related business."[42]

The analysis of whether a given arrangement involves illegal inducement is especially complex when a provider is paying a referral source to perform legitimate clinical, consulting, or other services. Ultimately, the question to be addressed is whether the provider is paying fair market value for needed services, or whether the provider is purchasing the referral source's services to induce referrals in violation of the AKS.

1.4.4.2   One Purpose Rule

Many courts of appeal—including the Third, Fifth, Seventh, Ninth, and Tenth Circuits—have employed a "one purpose" test to determine whether an arrangement is intended to induce referrals. This test was first articulated by the Third Circuit in *United States v. Greber*, where the court concluded that "if *one purpose* of the payment was to induce future referrals, the [AKS] has been violated."[43]

---

40. *Bay State*, 874 F.2d at 29.
41. Medicare and State Health Care Programs: Fraud and Abuse; OIG Anti-Kickback, 56 Fed. Reg. at 35,958 (citations omitted).
42. *Hanlester*, 51 F.3d at 1398.
43. United States v. Greber, 760 F.2d 68, 69 (3d Cir. 1985) (emphasis added); *accord* United States v. Davis, 132 F.3d 1092 (5th Cir. 1998) (finding that a jury may convict under the AKS if it finds the remuneration provided to an individual is "in part an inducement" to

In *Greber*, the defendant was a physician who was also the founder of a company that provided diagnostic services to physicians. One allegation was that the defendant paid referring physicians "interpretation fees" to compensate them for providing initial consultation services and for explaining initial test results to patients. However, there was evidence that the defendant had already evaluated the test data and that the fixed percentage payment to the referring physicians exceeded the amount allowed by Medicare for such services. As evidence, the government introduced testimony from a prior civil proceeding during which the defendant testified that "if the doctor didn't get his consulting fee, he wouldn't be using our service. So the doctor got a consulting fee."[44] Ultimately, the court found these payments violated the AKS, noting that if the payments were intended to induce the physician to order the company's diagnostic services, they were illegal even if the payments were also intended to compensate for professional services.[45]

Whether one purpose of offering or giving the remuneration was to induce referrals must be considered in the context of the AKS's scienter requirement. The relevant question is whether the one purpose must be a criminal purpose, as the AKS's language suggests. No court of appeals has directly answered this question. In *United States v. Davis*, a Fifth Circuit case that followed *Greber* in applying the one purpose test, the court addressed the issue of scienter and upheld the standard jury instruction that knowingly "means that the act was done voluntarily and intentionally, not because of mistake or accident," and willfully "means that the act was committed voluntarily and purposely with the specific intent to do something the law forbids; that is to say, with bad purpose either to disobey or disregard the law."[46] *Davis* also stands for the proposition that a jury may convict under the AKS if it finds the remuneration provided

---

refer patients); United States v. Borrasi, 639 F.3d 774 (7th Cir. 2011); United States v. Kats, 871 F.2d 105, 108 (9th Cir. 1989); United States v. McClatchey, 217 F.3d 823, 835 (10th Cir. 2000); United States v. LaHue, 261 F.3d 993 (10th Cir. 2001).
44. *Greber*, 760 F.2d at 70.
45. *Id.* at 72.
46. *Davis*, 132 F.3d at 1094.

to an individual is "in part an inducement" to refer.[47] Reading these two parts of *Davis* together, one can reasonably conclude that a jury may convict under the AKS only if it finds that remuneration was intentionally offered or given in part to induce referrals, with the knowledge that the conduct was unlawful.

Some circuit courts have taken a slightly different approach to analyzing "inducement." In *Bay State*, the First Circuit upheld the trial court's use of a "primary purpose" test. At issue in *Bay State* was a jury instruction given by the trial court that required the jury to find that inducement was the "primary purpose" of the payment and provided that no conviction could lie where that "improper purpose was an incidental or minor one in making payments."[48] The First Circuit commented that *Greber*'s "more expansive reading" of the AKS "implie[d] that the issue of the sole versus primary reason for payments [was] irrelevant since *any* amount of inducement [was] illegal."[49] Thus, the *Bay State* court found that it need not decide the exact reach of the AKS because "the district court instructed that the defendants could only be found guilty if the payments were made primarily as inducements [and at] a minimum this [comported] with congressional intent."[50]

Finally, two courts of appeal have explained that the AKS requires something more than the mere hope or expectation of referrals for inducement to be present. In *Hanlester*, a case involving physician-owned joint venture laboratories, the Ninth Circuit examined the private placement memoranda used to offer limited partnership shares in Hanlester's joint venture laboratories. The court found the essential marketing and structure of the joint venture lawful:

> The evidence shows that Hanlester desired to comply with the law and structured its business operation in a manner which it believed to be lawful. There is ample evidence that appellants

---

47. *See id.*
48. *Bay State*, 874 F.2d at 29.
49. *Id.* at 30.
50. *Id.*

intended to encourage limited partners to refer business to the joint venture laboratories. The appellants offered physicians the opportunity to profit indirectly from referrals when they could not profit directly. Potential partners were told that the success of the limited partnerships depended on referrals from the limited partners. While substantial cash distributions were made to limited partners by the joint venture labs, dividends were paid to limited partners based on each individual's ownership share of profits, and not on the volume of their referrals. Payments were made to limited partners whether or not they referred business to the joint venture labs.

The fact that a large number of referrals resulted in the potential for a high return on investment, or that the practical effect of low referral rates was failure for the labs, is insufficient to prove that appellants offered or paid remuneration to induce referrals.[51]

In contrast, the court found that Hanlester's vice president of marketing (1) implied to prospective physician limited partners that eligibility to purchase shares depended on an agreement to refer program-related business; (2) told prospective physician limited partners that the number of shares they could purchase in the joint venture labs would depend on the volume of their referrals to the labs; (3) stated that partners who did not refer business would be pressured to leave the partnerships; and (4) claimed that the partners' return on their investment would be virtually guaranteed.[52] Based on these findings, the court found that the vice president of marketing's conduct violated the AKS, thus making the Hanlester laboratories and general partner vicariously liable. Notably, even though the Ninth Circuit has adopted the one purpose test,[53] the *Hanlester* court never mentioned this theory.

---

51. *Hanlester*, 51 F.3d at 1399.
52. *Id.* at 1398.
53. *See Kats*, 871 F.2d at 108 (citing *Greber*, 760 F.2d at 69 (3d Cir. 1985)).

In *United States v. LaHue*, the Tenth Circuit adopted the one purpose rule, but took steps to avoid an extreme reading. It upheld the
district court's instruction to the jury that the defendant could not
"be convicted merely because [he] hoped or expected or believed
that referrals may ensue from remuneration that was designed wholly
for other purposes."[54] The court also observed that the application
of the AKS does not necessarily prohibit business relationships
"where the motivation to enter into the relationship [was] for legal
reasons entirely distinct from the collateral hope for or decision to
make referrals . . . [and] . . . [did] not make all conduct illegal [just
because the parties had] referrals in mind."[55]

1.4.5 Arranging for or Recommending

In addition to prohibiting the solicitation, receipt, offer, or payment
of remuneration in return for referrals of federal health care program
business, the AKS also criminalizes the solicitation, receipt, offer, or
payment of remuneration in return for arranging for or recommending certain items, including the leasing or purchasing of a facility
or goods, or the ordering of items or services payable by federal
health care program business. This prohibition can be referred to
as the second prong of the AKS.

A common example of an arrangement prohibited by the AKS's
second prong involves a broker-style relationship where the parties agree that one will arrange for or recommend referrals to the
other in exchange for a payment or something else of value. For
example, in *Modern Medical Laboratories v. Smith-Kline Beecham
Clinical Laboratories, Inc.*, a federal district court held that the second prong prohibited an agreement under which Modern Medical
Laboratories (MML) would market, manage, and operate a laboratory's business in return for 90 percent of its revenue.[56] MML argued
that it could not violate the AKS's first prong because only a physi-

---

54. *LaHue*, 261 F.3d at 1007.
55. *Id.* at 1008 (internal citations omitted).
56. Modern Med. Labs v. Smith-Kline Beecham Clinical Labs, Inc., No. 92-5302, 1994 U.S.
Dist. LEXIS 11525 (N.D. Ill. Aug. 16, 1994).

cian can order medical testing, which means that MML did not have the ability to refer. Without determining whether MML had violated the first prong, the court found that MML violated the second prong when it received remuneration from the laboratory in exchange for arranging for the purchase of services. The court found that under the second prong, "it is irrelevant that a physician made the initial decision to purchase certain testing services. . . . [The second prong] reaches activity whereby one entity receives remuneration for essentially taking a physician's 'order' for laboratory tests and arranging for another entity to perform the work."[57]

The Fourth Circuit similarly regarded commissions-based payments to contracted sales representatives as violating the AKS in *United States v. Mallory*.[58] Defendants—the owners of Health Diagnostic Laboratory (HDL) and a marketing company, BlueWave Healthcare Consultants (BlueWave)—entered into an arrangement whereby BlueWave marketed and sold HDL's tests in return for base pay plus sales commissions.[59] Defendants contended that they could not be liable for AKS violations because BlueWave's sales representatives did not directly refer testing to HDL.[60] The Fourth Circuit disagreed and instead found that "[the AKS] expressly prohibits individuals from receiving remuneration in exchange for 'arranging for or recommending purchasing' health care services. This includes sales representatives who are compensated for recommending a health care service, like the HDL . . . tests, to physicians."[61]

A Seventh Circuit case, *United States v. Polin*, concerns another common example of an arrangement that implicates the AKS's second prong.[62] In *Polin*, a sales representative sold pacemakers to hospitals and physicians, attended implant procedures, and ensured that patients were properly monitored after implantation. This last responsibility often required the sales representative to refer

---

57. *Id.* at *8.
58. United States v. Mallory, 988 F.3d 730 (4th Cir. 2021).
59. *Id.* at 735.
60. *Id.* at 738.
61. *Id.*
62. United States v. Polin, 194 F.3d 863 (7th Cir. 1999).

patients to an outside cardiac service for follow-up monitoring. If the physician chose to use such an outside service, the sales representative would contact that outside service, provide the patient's data, and ensure that the patient was set up for the proper monitoring.[63] Although the treating physician always had the right to refuse any outside service chosen, over the course of 14 years no physician had ever overruled the choice of the sales representative.[64]

The defendants in *Polin*—the physician director of an outside cardiac monitoring service and a nurse at the service—contacted the sales representative and offered him $50 cash for each Medicare patient he referred to the defendants' company for monitoring services.[65] The sales representative would receive no payment if the patient or physician refused to use the outside service, if the patient died before the monitoring services began, or if the patient was in a nursing home with which the defendants' company already had a monitoring contract. The sales representative questioned the legality of this offer and contacted the OIG, which worked with the sales representative to set up a sting operation.[66]

The defendant physician and nurse argued that "because the cardiac pacemaker patients at issue were referred by their respective physicians, not by [the sales representative]," the defendants did not violate the first prong of the AKS by offering payment to the sales representative.[67] The defendants did concede that they might have violated the second prong because they paid the sales representative to "recommend" to physicians that Medicare patients be sent to their company, but alleged that where the charges against them went only to the "refer" prong, they could not be found guilty. The Seventh Circuit rejected the defendants' assertion that the two prongs speak to "different and non-overlapping" conduct. The court stated that adopting such a view would lead to absurd results: only

---

63. *Id.* at 864–65.
64. *Id.* at 865.
65. *Id.* at 864.
66. *Id.* at 865.
67. *Id.*

a physician could violate the first prong as only he can "refer" a patient and only a layperson could violate the second prong since he can only "recommend" a particular service.[68] The court went on to state that these different provisions refer to the difference between referral of individuals (the first prong) and the recommendation of specific services (the second prong). The court concluded that this was a "classic case of an illegal kickback."[69] In exchange for directing Medicare patients to the outside service, the defendants were willing to, and did, pay the sales representative money.

In *Nursing Home Consultants v. Quantum Health Services, Inc.*, the U.S. District Court for the Eastern District of Arkansas found that a marketing agreement violated the AKS because a marketer of medical supplies (Nursing Home Consultants, NHC) was paid for referring and recommending Medicare recipients to a medical equipment supplier (Quantum).[70] Quantum engaged NHC to help broaden its sales base in the southwestern United States by identifying Medicare recipients who needed Quantum's medical supplies. NHC was supposed to put such recipients in contact with Quantum, so Quantum could then sell its products directly to nursing homes (on behalf of the residents).[71] NHC's annual compensation under the marketing agreement was to be determined on a per-item basis and was calculated based upon the number of units Quantum sold to those nursing home residents identified by NHC.[72] In other words, the more residents NHC referred to Quantum, the more money NHC made under the marketing agreement.

The case came before the court as a breach of contract action, but the court held that the marketing agreement was unenforceable because it violated the AKS, as NHC's compensation was directly tied to the sales numbers it generated for Quantum.[73] The court also

---

68. *Id.* at 866.
69. *Id.* at 867.
70. Nursing Home Consultants v. Quantum Health Servs., Inc., 926 F. Supp. 835 (E.D. Ark. 1996).
71. *Id.* at 839.
72. *Id.*
73. *Id.* at 847.

found the marketing agreement to be a violation of both the first and second prongs of the AKS because NHC was paid for both referring and recommending Medicare recipients to Quantum.[74]

1.4.6   Federal Health Care Program

The term "federal health care program" includes Medicare, all state Medicaid programs, and "any plan or program that provides health benefits, whether directly, through insurance, or otherwise, which is funded directly, in whole or in part, by the United States Government (other than the health insurance program under chapter 89 of title 5); or (2) any State health care program, as defined in section 1320a-7(h) of this title."[75] The broad reach of this definition includes TRICARE, the Veterans Administration, and block grant programs, but it does not cover the Federal Employee Health Benefits Program.

1.4.7   Referral

The AKS does not define "referring," as that term is used in the first prong of the AKS, but the Seventh Circuit has interpreted this term broadly to include signing a certification representing that a patient requires home health care even if the referring physician does not directly select which entity will provide the care. In *United States v. Patel*, a Chicago-area physician was convicted of referring patients to Grand Home Health Care (Grand) in exchange for undisclosed payments in violation of the AKS.[76] Even though Dr. Patel offered his patients various home health care provider options, his patients ultimately chose the provider, and they required such care, the district court held that Patel "referred" patients to Grand when he certified or recertified that the patient needed care to be provided by Grand.[77] On appeal, the Seventh Circuit found that a common meaning of "referral" is to provide an authorization for care, without specify-

---

74. *Id.* at 842–43.
75. 42 U.S.C. § 1320a-7b(f).
76. *See* United States v. Patel, 778 F.3d 607, 608–09 (7th Cir. 2015).
77. *Id.* at 609.

ing who provides it; Patel thus had "referred" patients to Grand in exchange for remuneration in violation of the AKS.[78] The Fifth Circuit adopted this holding in the 2017 case of *United States v. Dailey.*[79]

The Seventh Circuit revisited its interpretation of "referral" in a 2020 decision, stating expressly that "the definition of a referral under the [AKS] is broad, encapsulating both direct and indirect means of connecting a patient with a provider. It goes beyond explicit recommendations to include more subtle arrangements[,] [a]nd the inquiry is a practical one that focuses on substance, not form."[80] Other circuits have not delved deeply into the meaning of "referral" under the AKS. The Seventh Circuit's definition of "refer" is noteworthy because of its potential for overlap with the "arranging for or recommending" language in the second prong of the AKS.

1.5 Sanctions

An AKS violation can result in the imposition of a variety of criminal and civil sanctions. The AKS explicitly provides that a violation constitutes a felony that may carry a term of imprisonment of up to ten years. Violators may also be subject to fines of up to $100,000 for each violation.[81] In addition, violators may face civil penalties that are not articulated in the AKS, including civil monetary penalties and possible exclusion from federal health care programs. Violations of the AKS may also serve as the basis for a cause of action under the False Claims Act, which is explained in more detail in Chapter 5.

---

78. *Id.* at 613.
79. *See* United States v. Dailey, 868 F.3d 322, 330 (5th Cir. 2017) ("the issue is whether the [remuneration to the provider] for signing Form 485s can legally constitute a 'referral' of an individual for the purposes of furnishing a service for which payment may be made under Medicare. We conclude that it does.").
80. Stop Ill. Health Care Fraud, LLC v. Sayeed, 957 F.3d 743, 750 (7th Cir. 2020).
81. 42 U.S.C. § 1320a-7b(b). As discussed in Section 1.3, the Bipartisan Budget Act of 2018 increased the criminal penalties under the AKS from $25,000 to $100,000 and the maximum sentence from five years to ten years. Bipartisan Budget Act of 2018, Pub. L. No. 115-123, 132 Stat. 208, 220 (2018).

Since the late 1970s, Congress has mandated that the OIG exclude individuals or entities convicted of an AKS violation from participation in the federal health care programs.[82] In addition, in 1987 Congress granted the OIG discretionary authority to exclude individuals and entities for AKS violations that do not result in a conviction.[83] This discretionary authority provided a civil remedy alternative to criminal prosecution that would also address abusive business practices effectively.[84] In 1997, Congress expanded this authority by authorizing the OIG to impose civil monetary penalties for AKS violations.[85] In other words, Congress provided a mechanism for imposing penalties upon a showing of a mere preponderance of the evidence that the defendant engaged in prohibited conduct—and did not require proof of a violation of the criminal statute beyond a reasonable doubt. The new provision established penalties of $100,000 for each act committed in violation of the AKS and damages of up to three times the amount of the prohibited remuneration.[86]

Whether a party is subject to mandatory exclusion based on a conviction or permissive exclusion resulting from a case brought by the OIG, the excluded party has the right to appeal an exclusion and request a hearing before an administrative law judge, but only on the issues of whether (1) a basis for the imposition of the sanction existed or (2) the length of the exclusion was unreasonable in the case of a permissive exclusion only.[87] In the case of a permissive exclusion case brought by the OIG, a party has the opportunity to have the OIG hearing before imposition of the exclusion.

---

82. *See* Medicare-Medicaid Anti-Fraud and Abuse Amendments, Pub. L. No. 95-142, (1977); Social Security Act § 1128(a)(1), 42 U.S.C. § 1320a-7(a)(1).

83. Medicare and Medicaid Patient and Program Protection Act of 1987; Pub. L. No. 100-93, § 2, 101 Stat. 680, 680–86 (42 U.S.C. § 1320a-7(b)(7)).

84. *See* Medicare and State Health Care Programs: Fraud and Abuse; OIG Anti-Kickback, 56 Fed. Reg. 35,952 (July 29, 1991).

85. Balanced Budget Act of 1997, Pub. L. No. 105-33, § 4304(b), 111 Stat. 251, 383–84 (1997) (*reported at* 143 Cong. Rec. H6064 (July 29, 1997)).

86. *See* 42 U.S.C. § 1320a-7a.

87. *See* 42 C.F.R. § 1001.2007.

1.6 The OIG's Health Care Fraud Self-Disclosure Protocol

If a party determines that it may have violated the AKS, it can potentially mitigate its possible exposure by submitting a self-disclosure to the OIG pursuant to its Health Care Fraud Self-Disclosure Protocol (SDP), formerly named the Provider Self-Disclosure Protocol.[88] According to the OIG, disclosure can result in "significant benefits," such as a presumption against a corporate integrity agreement, release from permissive exclusion without requiring any integrity measures, and payment of a lower multiplier on single damages (which in no case would be less than one and a half times the single damages).[89]

Any health care provider, supplier, or other individual or entity subject to the OIG's civil monetary penalties authority may avail itself of the self-disclosure process. In addition to outlining the requirements applicable to all disclosures, the SDP provides specific guidance on AKS-related submissions. Among other things, the disclosing party must acknowledge that, in its reasonable assessment of the information available at the time of the disclosure, the arrangement at issue constituted a potential violation of the AKS. The self-disclosure must provide a narrative submission detailing the problematic arrangement, describe any corrective action taken to remedy the arrangement and any safeguards implemented to prevent the conduct from reoccurring, and offer a calculation of damages.

---

88. OIG's Health Care Fraud Self-Disclosure Protocol (updated Nov. 8, 2021), https://oig .hhs.gov/documents/self-disclosure-info/1006/Self-Disclosure-Protocol-2021.pdf.

89. *Id.* Between 1998 and 2020, the OIG resolved more than 2,200 disclosures resulting in recoveries of more than $870 million to federal health care programs. From 2016 to 2020, the OIG settled 330 disclosures, an increase from the 235 cases resolved from 2009 and 2013. Notably, the OIG reported that in all cases it released the disclosing parties from permissive exclusion without requiring any integrity measures, which offers some encouragement for entities considering submission of a self-disclosure to the OIG. *Id.*

The OIG revised the SDP on November 8, 2021. The revisions to the SDP included an increase to minimum settlement amounts required to resolve a matter from $50,000 to $100,000 for AKS-related matters and from $10,000 to $20,000 for all other matters.[90]

---

90. *Id.* The OIG also clarified that a disclosure must include itemized damages for each affected federal health care program and that the SDP can be used to report reportable events under corporate integrity agreements. The revised SDP also included minor changes regarding the OIG's coordination with the DOJ in criminal matters. Most notably, the OIG no longer encourages disclosure of potential criminal conduct through the SDP process or advocates to the DOJ for leniency in criminal cases.

Statutory Exceptions and Safe Harbors to the Anti-Kickback Statute

2

Shortly after enactment of the Anti-Kickback Statute (AKS), many in the health care industry began to express concern that innocuous or beneficial commercial arrangements could implicate the AKS and thus subject those involved to criminal or other sanctions. Although the AKS did not originally include any exceptions, Congress amended the statute in 1977 to include two statutory exceptions (discounts and payments to bona fide employees), in recognition of the breadth of transactions potentially implicated by the AKS. As discussed in Section 2.1, Congress has added various statutory exceptions through the years.[1]

In 1987, Congress again acknowledged the potential problems that could result from the breadth of the AKS's prohibition and directed the Office of Inspector General (OIG) to create "safe harbors" to specify certain business and payment practices that would be protected from prosecution under the AKS.[2] On July 29, 1991—almost four

---

1. 42 U.S.C. § 1320a-7b(b)(3).
2. *Id.* § 1320a-7b(b)(3)(E).

years after passage of the legislation requiring the creation of the safe harbors—the OIG finally issued the first set of final safe harbor regulations.[3] Since 1991, the OIG has promulgated additional safe harbors and has also clarified and amended the original safe harbors.[4] For example, in late November and early December 2020, the OIG published two final rules that amended existing safe harbors, created new safe harbors, and also modified or created definitions for key terms applicable to existing safe harbors.[5]

2.1 Statutory Exceptions

Congress has enacted statutory exceptions to the AKS for the following arrangements:

- Discounts
- Bona fide payments to W-2 employees
- Payments to purchasing agents (e.g., group purchasing organizations)
- Certain transactions that fit within regulatory safe harbors (see Section 2.2)
- Specified risk-sharing arrangements
- Waivers or reductions by pharmacies of any Medicare Part D beneficiary cost-sharing amounts
- Certain payments between a federally qualified health center and a Medicare Advantage organization
- Payments that allow certain health care entities to maintain, increase, or enhance the quality of services provided to medically underserved populations

---

3. *See* 56 Fed. Reg. 35,952 (July 29, 1991). These early safe harbors addressed the following types of arrangements: investment interests, space rental, equipment rental, personal services and management contracts, sale of practice, referral services, warranties, discounts, employees, and group purchasing organizations.
4. *See* 57 Fed. Reg. 52,723 (Nov. 5, 1992); 61 Fed. Reg. 2122 (Jan. 25, 1996); 64 Fed. Reg. 63,518 (Nov. 19, 1999); 66 Fed. Reg. 62,979 (Dec. 4, 2001); 71 Fed. Reg. 45,110 (Aug. 8, 2006); 72 Fed. Reg. 56,632 (Oct. 4, 2007); 78 Fed. Reg. 79,202 (Dec. 27, 2013); 81 Fed. Reg. 88,368 (Dec. 7, 2016); 85 Fed. Reg. 76,666 (Nov. 30, 2020); 85 Fed. Reg. 77,684 (Dec. 2, 2020).
5. 85 Fed. Reg. 76,666 (Nov. 30, 2020); 85 Fed. Reg. 77,684 (Dec. 2, 2020).

- Prescription drug discounts for certain beneficiaries in the Medicare Part D "coverage gap" or "doughnut hole"
- Incentive payments made to certain Medicare beneficiaries under accountable care organization beneficiary incentive programs[6]

A detailed discussion of the statutory exceptions is beyond the scope of this publication, but some are discussed in the context of their corresponding regulatory safe harbors in Section 2.2.

2.2 Safe Harbors

Since 1991, the OIG has promulgated a number of regulatory safe harbors.[7] A business transaction or arrangement that satisfies every element of a safe harbor is immunized from prosecution. If a transaction or arrangement does not satisfy every element of a relevant safe harbor, it is not per se illegal. In this situation, the OIG will assess the arrangement to determine whether, based on the facts and circumstances particular to the arrangement, the potential risk of fraud and abuse is sufficiently low.

In evaluating whether a particular arrangement violates the AKS, the OIG generally looks to whether the arrangement has the potential to:

- increase costs to federal health care programs, beneficiaries, or enrollees;
- increase the risk of overutilization or inappropriate utilization;
- result in unfair competition by freezing out competitors unwilling to pay kickbacks; or
- interfere with appropriate clinical decision-making.[8]

The likelihood of enforcement under the AKS depends on numerous factors, including whether a safe harbor does not exist to capture

---

6. 42 U.S.C. § 1320a-7b(b)(3).
7. *See* 42 C.F.R. § 1001.952.
8. *See* OIG Special Advisory Bulletin on Contractual Joint Ventures, 68 Fed. Reg. 23,148 (Apr. 30, 2003).

an otherwise innocuous arrangement, whether a good-faith effort was made to comply with the safe harbor requirements, and whether the arrangement was intended to induce referrals.[9]

The following is a list of all of the current safe harbors:

1. Investment interests in large publicly traded entities or certain small entities
2. Space rentals
3. Equipment rentals
4. Personal services and management contracts and outcomes-based payment arrangements
5. Sale of practice
6. Referral services
7. Warranties
8. Discounts
9. Employees
10. Group purchasing organizations
11. Waivers of certain beneficiary copayment, coinsurance, and deductible amounts
12. Increased coverage, reduced cost-sharing amounts, or reduced premium amounts offered by certain health plans
13. Price reductions offered to certain health plans
14. Rural practitioner recruitment incentives
15. Obstetrical malpractice insurance subsidies
16. Investment interests in group practices composed exclusively of active investors who are licensed health care professionals
17. Cooperative hospital service organizations
18. Investment interests in surgeon-owned, single-specialty, multi-specialty, and hospital/physician ambulatory surgical centers (ASCs)
19. Referral arrangements for specialty services
20. Price reductions offered to eligible managed care organizations
21. Price reductions offered by contractors with substantial financial risk to qualified managed care plans

---

9. *See* 56 Fed. Reg. at 35,954.

22. Ambulance replenishment arrangements
23. Federally qualified health centers
24. Electronic prescribing items and services
25. Electronic health records items and services
26. Agreements between federally qualified health centers and Medicare Advantage organizations
27. Drug pricing discounts to beneficiaries under the Medicare Gap Coverage Discount Program
28. Free or discounted local transportation to federal health care program beneficiaries
29. Care coordination arrangements between value-based enterprise participants and/or value-based enterprises to improve quality, health outcomes, and efficiency
30. Value-based arrangements with substantial downside financial risk
31. Value-based arrangements with full financial risk
32. Arrangements for patient engagement and support to improve quality, health outcomes, and efficiency
33. CMS-sponsored model arrangements and CMS-sponsored model patient incentives
34. Cybersecurity technology and related services
35. Accountable care organization beneficiary incentive programs

The required elements of each safe harbor are found at 42 C.F.R. § 1001.952. The most commonly used safe harbors are discussed next in Section 2.3.

2.3 Commonly Used Safe Harbors

2.3.1 Space and Equipment Rentals

The space and equipment rental safe harbors arise most often in arrangements between providers and referring physicians.[10] Although set forth as two separate safe harbors, the requirements of each are

---

10. 42 C.F.R. § 1001.952(b) and (c).

substantially the same. To qualify for protection under any of these safe harbors, an arrangement must meet the following criteria:

- The agreement must be set out in writing and signed by the parties.
- The agreement must specify all of the premises/equipment leased between the parties for the term of the lease, and also specify the premises/equipment covered by the lease.
- If the agreement is intended to provide for access to the premises/use of the equipment for periodic intervals of time (rather than on a full-time basis), the agreement must specify the schedule of such intervals, their precise length, and the exact charge for each interval.
- The term of the agreement must be for at least one year.
- The aggregate rental charge paid over the term of the agreement must be set in advance, be consistent with fair market value in arm's-length transactions, and not be determined in a manner that takes into account the volume or value of any referrals or business otherwise generated between the parties, for which payment may be made (in whole or in part) by Medicare, Medicaid, or other federal health care programs.
- The aggregate space/equipment rented does not exceed that which is reasonably necessary to accomplish the commercially reasonable business purpose of the rental arrangement.[11]

One of the most important elements of these safe harbors is the fair market value requirement.[12] With respect to space rentals, the safe harbor explains that "fair market value" means the value of the rental property for "general commercial purposes."[13] In other words, a rental payment cannot be "adjusted to reflect the additional value that one party . . . would attribute to the property as a result of its proximity or convenience to sources of referrals or business other-

---

11. *Id.*
12. *Id.* § 1001.952(b)(6), (c)(6).
13. *Id.* § 1001.952(b)(6).

wise generated for which payment may be made in whole or in part by Medicare, Medicaid, and all other Federal health care programs" and still meet the "fair market value" requirement.[14]

The safe harbor for equipment rentals includes similar language with respect to the meaning of fair market value in that context: "the value of equipment when obtained from a manufacturer or professional distributor."[15] Like the space rental safe harbor, this definition of fair market value excludes adjustments to reflect additional value that a party might attribute based on proximity or convenience to sources of referrals or other federal health care program business.

To ensure that payments are fair market value, the safest course of action is to obtain an independent third-party valuation for each referral source arrangement. If a valuation for each arrangement is not practical or cost effective, the parties should carefully document their discussions and methodology in arriving at the payment amount and ensure that the payment does not in any way reflect the volume or value of referrals or other business generated between the parties.

Two of the other common elements of these safe harbors present practical difficulties: that the aggregate compensation be set in advance and that the agreement set forth the exact intervals and exact charges for each interval if space or equipment are provided on a part-time basis. For example, the OIG has stated that a part-time or as-needed service arrangement involving a compensation formula based on an hourly rate does not fully satisfy the set-in-advance requirement of the personal services safe harbor.[16] Space rental and equipment rental arrangements involving percentage-based, per-unit, or per-click payments also do not meet the set-in-advance requirement.[17] Additionally, while acknowledging the practical difficulties in meeting the set-in-advance requirement and specifying

---

14. *Id.*
15. *Id.* § 1001.952(c)(6).
16. 64 Fed. Reg. 63,518, 63,526 (Nov. 19, 1999).
17. *See* OIG Adv. Op. 08-10 (Aug. 26, 2008); OIG Adv. Op. 03-08 (Apr. 10, 2003); OIG Adv. Op. 11-15 (Oct. 11, 2011).

detailed use schedules for part-time or as-needed arrangements, the OIG has declared that these requirements are necessary to ensure that safe harbor protection is not afforded to arrangements that include payments adjusted periodically on the basis of the volume or value of referrals.[18] At the same time, the OIG emphasized that an arrangement that does not comply fully with a safe harbor is not per se illegal and that there may be instances where part-time, as-needed, and other similar arrangements are lawful.[19]

Although one of the simplest elements of these safe harbors, the one-year-term requirement often bumps up against legitimate business concerns if the parties do not want the arrangement to continue for a full year or if the parties need to terminate the arrangement prior to the end of the first year. According to the OIG, the one-year-term requirement ensures that protected leases or contracts cannot be readjusted more frequently based on the number of referrals between the parties.[20] Agreements may include provisions allowing termination for cause and still satisfy the one-year-term requirement but only if the for-cause termination provision (1) specifies the conditions giving rise to termination and (2) prohibits renegotiation of the agreement or further financial arrangements between the parties for the duration of the one-year term.[21] Agreements containing without-cause termination provisions do not comply with the one-year-term requirement, even if the agreement prohibits renegotiation of the agreement or further financial arrangements between the parties for the duration of the one-year term.[22] In drawing the line between for-cause and without-cause termination provisions, the OIG has indicated that without-cause termination provisions could allow parties to disguise payments for referrals by terminating an agreement after payment is made but before any services are performed.[23] The one-year prohibition on renegotiation or further

---

18. *See* 64 Fed. Reg. 63,526.
19. *Id.*
20. *Id.*
21. *Id.*
22. *Id.*
23. *See id.*

financial arrangements between the parties would not effectively prevent such abuses.[24]

In 1999, the OIG amended the space and equipment rental safe harbors (among others) to provide that the arrangements must be based upon a "commercially reasonable business purpose" as opposed to a "legitimate business purpose." In the preamble to the final rule, the OIG stated that the "commercially reasonable business purpose" test is intended to preclude safe harbor protection for health care providers that "surreptitiously pay for referrals . . . by renting more space or equipment or purchasing more services than they actually need from referral sources."[25]

The OIG has rarely addressed the space, equipment, and personal services safe harbors outside of regulatory preambles and OIG advisory opinions. In 2000, however, the OIG issued a special fraud alert regarding the rental of space in physician offices by persons or entities to which the physicians refer.[26] As discussed in Section 4.3, the OIG issues special fraud alerts and advisory bulletins to identify suspect practices that are subject to scrutiny under the AKS. In this particular special fraud alert, the OIG expressed concern with the proliferation of space leases between physicians and the entities to which they refer and provided the following examples of suspect rental arrangements:

- Rental amounts that are not fair market value or that vary with the number of patients or referrals
- Rental amounts that are subject to modification more often than annually or arrangements that are on an "as needed" basis
- Rental amounts for space that is unnecessary or not used and nonexclusive occupancy arrangements.

---

24. *Id.*
25. *See* 64 Fed. Reg. 63,526.
26. OIG Special Fraud Alert, Rental of Space in Physician Offices by Persons or Entities to Which Physicians Refer, 65 Fed. Reg. 9274 (Feb. 24, 2000).

2.3.2 Personal Service Arrangements and Management Contracts and Outcomes-Based Payment Arrangements

Another commonly used safe harbor protects personal services arrangements and management contracts. Effective January 19, 2021, the OIG amended this safe harbor to also protect outcomes-based payment arrangements and to more closely align with the Stark Law exception for personal services arrangements.[27] These changes also arguably made the safe harbor requirements easier to satisfy.

Generally speaking, for personal services arrangements and management contracts to achieve safe harbor protection: (1) the arrangement at issue must be set out in writing and signed by the parties, last for a term of at least one year, cover all services to be provided over the term of the agreement, and specify what those services are; (2) the methodology for determining the compensation paid over the term of the agreement must be set in advance, consistent with fair market value in arm's-length transactions, and not be determined in a manner that takes into account the volume or value of any referrals or business otherwise generated between the parties for which payment may be made in whole or in part under applicable federal health care programs; (3) the services performed under the agreement must not involve the counseling or promotion of a business arrangement or other activity that violates state or federal law; and (4) the aggregate services contracted for must not exceed those that are reasonably necessary to accomplish the commercially reasonable business purpose of the services.

Through the 2020 final rule that explained the 2021 amendments, the OIG made two important changes to this safe harbor. First, the OIG eliminated the requirement that an agreement involving services on a periodic, sporadic, or part-time basis must specify the schedule, length, and exact charge for such intervals. Even though the OIG has a long-standing concern about part-time arrangements, because they can be easily modified based on referral patterns, it has determined

---

27. *See* 42 C.F.R. §§ 411,354(d), 411.357(d).

that other safeguards (e.g., the compensation methodology being set in advance at fair market value and commercially reasonable) are sufficient to protect against fraud and abuse. Second, the requirement that aggregate compensation be set in advance has been replaced with a requirement that the *methodology* for determining compensation be set in advance. This significant change—which is consistent with the Stark Law exception—allows arrangements to comply with this safe harbor even if, for example, compensation is set on an hourly basis. The OIG's view is that other compensation-related requirements (e.g., fair market value, commercial reasonableness, and the prohibition against taking into account the volume or value of referrals) mitigate against risk of parties periodically adjusting compensation to reward referrals.

Finally, as part of the 2020 final rule, the OIG added to this safe harbor protections for outcomes-based payment arrangements in response to the many new value-based payment models.[28] Outcomes-based payments are defined as payments that (1) reward a recipient for successfully achieving outcome measures or (2) reduce payments to a recipient for failing to achieve outcome measures.[29] Outcome measures must be selected based on clinical evidence or credible medical support and must be used to quantify quality improvements, reductions in payor costs, or both.[30]

2.3.3 Employees

Compared to independent contractor arrangements, which must comply with the more onerous personal services safe harbor requirements to be fully protected from prosecution, bona fide employee relationships are subject to few requirements under the employee safe harbor. The employee safe harbor protects any amounts paid by an employer to a bona fide employee for the furnishing of any item or service for which payment may be made in whole or in part under Medicare, Medicaid, or other federal health care programs.[31]

---

28. 42 C.F.R. § 1001.952(d)(2).
29. *Id.* § 1001.952(d)(3)(ii).
30. *Id.* § 1001.952(d)(2)(i).
31. *Id.* § 1001.952(i).

For purposes of the employee safe harbor, "employee" has the same meaning as it does under 26 U.S.C. § 3121(d)(2), which defines an employee, in relevant part, as any officer of a corporation or any individual who, under the usual common law rules applicable in determining the employer-employee relationship, has the status of an employee.[32] The OIG has taken the position that the exemption for payments made by an employer to an employee does not extend to independent contractors paid on a commission basis.[33]

2.3.4   Small Entity Investment Interests/ ASC Investments

When the OIG developed the original set of safe harbors, health care providers expressed broad support for a safe harbor that would protect physician ownership and joint venture arrangements in non-publicly traded companies. In response, the OIG promulgated the small entity investment interests safe harbor.[34] Under this safe harbor, investors are divided into two classes—"tainted" (or interested) investors who are in a position to refer patients, items, or services or otherwise generate business for the entity and "untainted" investors who hold an investment interest but do no business with the entity.

The two most important elements of the small entity investment interests safe harbor are commonly referred to as the 60–40 investor rule and the 60–40 revenue rule. Under the 60–40 investor rule, tainted investors can hold no more than 40 percent of the investment interests.[35] The safe harbor allows equivalent classes of equity investments and debt instruments to be combined in order to apportion investors into tainted and untainted pools for purposes of meeting the 60–40 investor rule.[36] Classes of investment interests may be combined when (1) the investors have similar rights with respect to the entity's income and assets, (2) the investors receive equiva-

---

32. 26 U.S.C. § 3121(d)(2).
33. 54 Fed. Reg. 3088 (Jan. 23, 1989).
34. 42 C.F.R. § 1001.952(a)(2).
35. *Id.* § 1001.952(a)(2)(i).
36. *Id.*

lent returns in proportion to their investments, and (3) there is no preferential treatment of referral source investors in connection with the disposition of the entity's assets.[37] The OIG has explicitly stated that, for purposes of meeting the 60–40 investor rule, tainted investors may include not only physicians but also hospitals, nursing homes, skilled nursing facilities, managed care companies, physician practice plans, manufacturers, or other institutions in a position to refer patients, products, or services to the entity.[38]

Under the 60–40 revenue rule, no more than 40 percent of the entity's gross revenue related to the furnishing of health care items and services may come from referrals or business otherwise generated from investors.[39] In the 1999 safe harbor regulations, the OIG clarified that only assets or revenues related to the furnishing of "health care items or services" will be counted for purposes of qualifying for the 60–40 revenue rule.[40] In this context, "health care items and services" means (1) health care items, devices, supplies, and services, and (2) items or services reasonably related to the furnishing of health care items, devices, supplies, or services, including but not limited to nonemergency transportation, patient education, attendant services, social services, utilization review, quality assurance, and practice management services.[41]

Other requirements of the safe harbor include the following:

- The investment terms for a tainted investor must be no different than those offered to an untainted investor.
- The investment terms must not be related to the expected value or volume of referrals.
- The investment terms may not require that an investor make referrals to the entity.

---

37. 64 Fed. Reg. at 63,523.
38. *Id.*
39. 42 C.F.R. § 1001.952(a)(2)(vi).
40. 64 Fed. Reg. at 63,522.
41. *Id.*

- All marketing of the entity's items or services must be on the same terms to investors as to noninvestors.
- Neither the entity nor any investor may loan funds to or guarantee a loan for a tainted investor for the purpose of using any part of the loan proceeds to purchase an investment interest in the entity.
- The return on the investment interest must be proportionate to the amount of capital contributed by the investor.

The OIG has also published significant guidance on physician investment arrangements. In 1989, three years before promulgating the small entity investment interests safe harbor, the OIG issued a special fraud alert on joint venture arrangements[42] identifying the elements of "suspect" physician joint ventures. While the OIG acknowledged that there may be legitimate reasons to form a joint venture, the OIG warned that some joint ventures may violate the AKS by serving to "lock up a stream of referrals from the physician investors and to compensate them indirectly for these referrals."[43] The OIG noted that suspect joint ventures may include (1) choosing investors because they are in a position to make referrals; (2) physician investments that are disproportionately small, as compared to their investment returns; (3) physician investors who invest only a nominal amount in the joint venture; and (4) physician investors who are permitted to borrow the amount of their investment from the entity and pay it back through deductions from profit distributions, thus eliminating the need to contribute cash. The subsequent safe harbor addresses many of the OIG's initial concerns with physician investments in entities to which the physicians are in a position to refer.

Then, in 1999, in response to growing concerns about the inability of physicians and hospitals to invest in ambulatory surgery centers (ASCs), the OIG promulgated a safe harbor to protect physician and

---

42. *See* OIG Special Fraud Alert on Joint Venture Arrangements, 59 Fed. Reg. 65,373–74 (Dec. 19, 1994).
43. *Id.*

hospital ownership of Medicare-certified ASCs.[44] Unlike physician joint ventures in other entities, the OIG wanted to encourage physician investment in ASCs because ASCs were viewed as having the potential to lower health care costs to the government. The ASC safe harbor is thus more liberal than the small investment interests safe harbor. For example, instead of limiting physician investors to a minority interest in the ASC, the ASC safe harbor allows physicians to own up to 100 percent. Additionally, up to 100 percent of the ASC's gross revenues may come from physician investors. The safe harbor also *requires* that at least one-third of each physician investor's medical practice income be derived from the physician's performance of surgical procedures at the ASC.

In 2003, the OIG issued a special advisory bulletin highlighting its concerns about certain types of "contractual joint venture" arrangements in which there is no formal investment entity but that may potentially reward health care providers for referrals.[45] In the advisory bulletin, the OIG focused on those arrangements in which a health care provider expands into a related health care business by contracting with an existing provider or supplier of a related item or service, and the health care provider is in a position to make patient referrals to the new business.

Additionally, in March 2013, the OIG issued a special fraud alert critical of physician investment activity in medical device distributors (i.e., physician-owned distributors, or PODs).[46] In this alert, the OIG reiterated its long-standing concern regarding any arrangement that gives a referring physician the ability to profit from referrals, including physician investment in an entity for which the physician generates business. The OIG identified four major concerns with PODs: (1) corruption of medical judgment; (2) overutilization; (3) increased costs to federal health care programs and beneficiaries;

---

44. *See* 64 Fed. Reg. 63,518 (Nov. 19, 1999); 42 C.F.R. § 1001.952(r).
45. *See* OIG Special Advisory Bulletin on Contractual Joint Ventures (Apr. 2003).
46. *See* OIG Special Fraud Alert on Physician-Owned Entities (Mar. 26, 2013), http://oig .hhs.gov/fraud/docs/alertsandbulletins/2013/POD_Special_Fraud_Alert.pdf.

and (4) unfair competition. The OIG dismisses patient disclosure as being sufficient to address these concerns.

2.3.5 Discounts

The AKS includes both a statutory exception and regulatory safe harbor that protects certain discounts. But, before analyzing the intricacies of this exception and safe harbor, one should consider whether a given arrangement even implicates the AKS, as the statute does not criminalize the normal buying and selling of facilities, goods, or services. As we discuss in Subsection 1.4.2, the flow of remuneration is critical to the analysis of whether an arrangement implicates the AKS. In the context of discounts, the potentially illegal remuneration is not the price a buyer pays to the seller for the good or service, but instead is the discount or reduction in price that the seller offers a buyer.

The discount exception protects "a discount or other reduction in price obtained by a provider of services or other entity under a Federal health care program if the reduction in price is *properly disclosed* and *appropriately reflected* in the costs claimed or charges made by the provider or entity under a Federal health care program."[47]

According to the legislative history, Congress enacted the discount exception to ensure that providers could seek discounts as part of a business transaction, which would result in savings to the Medicare and Medicaid programs.[48]

In 1991, the OIG promulgated a regulatory safe harbor for purchasing discounts received by providers.[49] In so doing, the OIG noted that the purpose of the discount safe harbor is to interpret the statutory exception.[50] Unlike the simply stated statutory discount exception,

---

47. 42 U.S.C. § 1320a-7b(b)(3)(A) (emphasis added).
48. H.R. Rep. No. 95-393(II), at 53, *reprinted in* 1977 U.S.C.C.A.N 3039, 3056.
49. 42 C.F.R. § 1001.952(h).
50. OIG Adv. Op. 13-07 (July 1, 2013), at 4; *see also* 56 Fed. Reg. 35,952 (July 29, 1991); 64 Fed. Reg. 63,518 (Nov. 19, 1999).

the discount safe harbor sets forth a lengthy and technical set of definitions and requirements.

To qualify for protection under the discount safe harbor, a transaction must (1) meet the regulatory definition of a discount and (2) be disclosed and reported, as applicable. The discount safe harbor establishes separate disclosure obligations for different types of entities (i.e., buyers, sellers, and offerors), and within each of these categories the reporting and disclosure requirements depend on the type of reimbursement to which the purchasing provider is subject.[51]

The safe harbor defines a discount as "a reduction in the amount a buyer (who buys either directly or through a wholesaler or a group purchasing organization) is charged for an item or service based on an arms-length transaction," including rebates.[52]

The OIG's definition of a protected discount under the safe harbor specifically excludes the following:

---

51. In *United States v. Shaw*, the court read the statutory language that a discount had to be "properly disclosed and appropriately reflected in the costs claimed or charges made by the provider or entity under a federal health care program" to mean that the discount exception applied to those who accept and those who offer discounts and thus "[b]oth buyer-providers and seller-suppliers are required to 'properly disclose and appropriately reflect' the reduction in price [to Medicare and Medicaid] in order to avoid criminal liability." 106 F. Supp. 2d 103, 119–20 (D. Mass. 2000). This interpretation of the statutory exception is at odds with the discount safe harbor in two important ways. First, the discount safe harbor gives separate protection to buyers, sellers, and offerors irrespective of whether the other party complies. Second, only cost report buyers must disclose to the Medicare and Medicaid programs the discounts received.

52. 42 C.F.R. § 1001.952(h)(5). "Rebates" are defined as any discount that is not given at the time of sale so long as the terms of the rebate "are fixed and disclosed in writing to the buyer at the time of the initial purchase to which the discount applies." 42 C.F.R. § 1001.952(h)(4). Although the discount safe harbor does not explicitly require that the rebate *only* be paid subsequent to the sale, the OIG has taken the position that "prebates" cannot qualify for protection under the safe harbor because the monies are paid before any purchase and are not tied to the purchase of specific products. July 17, 2000, Letter from D. McCarty Thornton, Chief Counsel to the Inspector General. Additionally, in 2003, the OIG opined that a "prebate" is one form of remuneration that implicates the AKS. OIG Compliance Guidance for Pharmaceutical Manufacturers, 68 Fed. Reg. 23,731, 23,736 (May 5, 2003) ("[A]ny remuneration from a manufacturer provided to a purchaser that is expressly or impliedly related to a sale potentially implicates the anti-kickback statute and should be carefully reviewed. Examples of remuneration in connection with a sale include, but are not limited to, 'prebates' and 'upfront payments,' other free or reduced-price goods or services, and payments to cover the costs of 'converting' from a competitor's product.").

- Cash payment or cash equivalents (except that rebates may be in the form of a check)
- A reduction in price applicable to one payer but not to Medicare, Medicaid, or other federal health care programs
- A routine reduction or waiver of any coinsurance or deductible amount owed by a program beneficiary
- Warranties
- Services provided in accordance with a personal or management services contract
- Other remuneration, in cash or in kind, not explicitly described in this section[53]

Effective January 1, 2026, this safe harbor will also exclude from the definition of protected discounts reductions in price in connection with the sale or purchase of prescription drugs from manufacturers to Medicare Part D plan sponsors, either directly or through pharmacy benefit managers acting under contract with them, unless the reduction is required by law.[54] However, the fate of this regulatory change remains uncertain. At press time, pending federal legislation contains a provision that would prohibit OIG from implementing this rule.[55]

In the 1991 final rule implementing the discount safe harbor, the OIG specifically considered and rejected imposition of a requirement that a buyer must pass along the benefit of discounts to federal health care programs to qualify for protection under the discount safe harbor.[56] Indeed, buyers that do not share substantial risk or fur-

---

53. 42 C.F.R. § 1001.952(h)(5).
54. Fraud and Abuse, Removal of Safe Harbor Protection for Rebates Involving Prescription Pharmaceuticals and Creation of New Safe Harbor Protection for Certain Point-of-Sale Reductions in Price on Pharmaceuticals and Certain Pharmacy Benefit Manager Service Fees, 85 Fed. Reg. 76,666, 76,667 (Nov. 30, 2020) (however, reductions in price negotiated between manufacturers and plan sponsors under Part D (or through PBMs under contract with the plan sponsors) in the form of upfront discounts, rather than after-sale rebates, are eligible for protection under a new safe harbor for point-of-sale reductions in price for prescription pharmaceutical products at § 1001.952(cc)).
55. *See* Build Back Better Act, H.R. 5376, § 139301.
56. *See* 56 Fed. Reg. 35,952 (July 29, 1991).

nish cost reports to the Centers for Medicare and Medicaid Services (CMS) are not even obligated to report the amount of the discount on their claims to Medicare.[57] Notably, however, and notwithstanding this clearly articulated position of the OIG, several courts have found that discounts not passed through to the Medicare and Medicaid programs constitute remuneration under the AKS.[58]

2.3.6 Managed Care

In 1996, Congress recognized the need to protect certain arrangements between managed care entities and their contracted health care providers that could potentially lower health care costs. Thus, as part of the Health Insurance Portability and Accountability Act, Congress enacted a statutory exception to the AKS for shared risk arrangements between managed care organizations and their contracted providers.[59] That same year, the OIG finalized the commonly used safe harbor protecting certain negotiated price reduction agreements between health plans and their contracted providers.[60]

The safe harbor protecting price reductions offered to health plans recognizes that contracted health care providers typically offer a reduction in their usual fees to health plans such as health maintenance organizations and preferred provider organizations in return for the providers obtaining a large volume of patients. The requirements that must be met to qualify for protection under this safe harbor are different depending on the type of health plan involved in the arrangement.[61]

---

57. 42 C.F.R. § 1001.952(h)(1)(iii).
58. *See* United States v. Shaw, 106 F. Supp. 2d 103 (D. Mass. 2000); Klaczak v. Consol. Med. Transp., 458 F. Supp. 2d 622 (N.D. Ill. 2006).
59. Pub. L. No. 104-191, § 216.
60. 42 C.F.R. § 1001.952(m).
61. The safe harbor for price reductions offered to health plans applies only to "contract health care providers" who are individuals or entities under contract to a health plan to furnish to the health plan's enrollees items or services that are covered by the health plan, Medicare, or a state health care program. Although such health care providers may have contractual relationships with health plans to perform a variety of other functions, such as marketing or peer review, "the term 'contract health care provider' . . . is limited to contractual relations for the furnishing of covered items and services." 57 Fed. Reg. 52,725 (Nov. 5, 1992).

The safe harbor protects price reductions between contracted providers and risk-based health plans under contract with CMS or a state Medicaid agency as long as the burden of the price reduction is not shifted to other payors, individuals, Medicare, or a state health care program.[62] Health plans under contract with CMS or a state Medicaid agency that receive payment on a reasonable cost or similar basis must meet additional requirements.[63]

Reductions in price offered to commercial health plans that pay contracted health care providers for services provided to enrollees on any basis other than at-risk capitation (e.g., fee-for-service) may qualify for safe harbor protection if the health plan and the contracted health care provider meet the following requirements:

- The fee schedule contained in the agreement between the health plan and the contracted health care provider must remain in effect throughout the term of the agreement, unless a fee increase results directly from a payment update authorized by Medicare or the state health care program.
- The party submitting claims or requests for payment from Medicare or the state health care program for items and services furnished in accordance with the agreement must not claim or request payment for amounts in excess of the fee schedule.[64]

The final category of this safe harbor applies to pricing arrangements offered by contracted health care providers to commercial health plans pursuant to which the contracted health care provider is compensated on an at-risk capitated basis. To qualify for safe harbor protection, the arrangement must comply with the four requirements for non-risk-based health plans under contract with CMS or a state Medicaid agency. Additionally, the payment amount contained in the agreement between the health care plan and the contracted

---

62. 42 C.F.R. § 1001.952(m)(1)(i).
63. *Id.* § 1001.952(m)(1)(ii).
64. *Id.* § 1001.952(m)(1)(iii).

health care provider must remain in effect throughout the term of the agreement.[65]

2.3.7 Electronic Health Records

In 2006, the OIG adopted the electronic health records (EHR) technology donation safe harbor, which was intended to promote the adoption and use of EHR.[66] This safe harbor allows entities to provide cost-sharing assistance to health care providers installing EHR systems without running afoul of the AKS.[67] At the time it was enacted, this safe harbor was unique because unlike other safe harbors it included a sunset provision.[68] The OIG originally decided to sunset this safe harbor as of December 31, 2013, based on its belief that "the need for a safe harbor for donations of [EHR would] diminish substantially over time as the use of such technology [became] a standard and expected part of medical practice."[69] The OIG later extended the sunset date to December 31, 2021, and then eliminated the sunset altogether in amendments that took effect in January 2021.[70]

The EHR donation safe harbor requires that each arrangement be set forth in a written agreement between the donor and recipient,[71] and the arrangement is protected only if the recipient covers at least 15 percent of the cost of the technology and related services, such as training, help desk, and maintenance services.[72] In addition, any updates, upgrades, or modifications to the donated technology that are not covered under the initial purchase price are subject to

---

65. *Id.* § 1001.952(m)(1)(iv).
66. *Id.* § 1001.952(y).
67. *Id.*
68. Medicare and State Health Care Programs: Fraud and Abuse; Safe Harbors for Certain Electronic Prescribing and Electronic Health Records Arrangements under the Anti-Kickback Statute, 71 Fed. Reg. 45,110 (Aug. 8, 2006).
69. Medicare and State Health Care Programs: Fraud and Abuse; Electronic Health Records under the Anti-Kickback Statute, 78 Fed. Reg. 79,202, 79,206 (Dec. 27, 2013).
70. *Id.* at 79,202; Medicare and State Health Care Programs: Fraud and Abuse; Revisions to Safe Harbors Under the Anti-Kickback Statute and Civil Monetary Penalty Rules Regarding Beneficiary Inducement, 85 Fed. Reg. 77,684, 77,830 (Dec. 2, 2020).
71. 42 C.F.R. § 1001.952(y)(6).
72. *Id.* § 1001.952(y)(11).

a separate cost-sharing obligation. The donor may not finance the recipient's cost-sharing obligation or loan funds to the recipient to pay for the recipient's portion of the donated technology.[73] There is no cap on the amount of protected technology that can be donated.

The potential class of donors and recipients for EHR technology is quite broad, but as a result of changes made in 2013, it includes a notable exception. Under the safe harbor, "any individual or entity, *other than a laboratory company*, that provides covered services and submits claims or requests for payment, either directly or through reassignment, to any federal health care program, and health plans" may qualify as a protected donor or recipient.[74] When the OIG amended the EHR donation safe harbor on December 27, 2013, it explicitly excluded laboratory companies in part in response to "concerns articulated by commenters and the wide-ranging support from the entire spectrum of the laboratory industry (from small, pathologist-owned laboratory companies to a national laboratory trade association that represents the industry's largest laboratory companies)."[75] While the OIG explained that its decision was "consistent with and further[ed] the goal of promoting the adoption of interoperable electronic health record technology that benefits patient care while reducing the likelihood that the safe harbor [would be] misused by donors to secure referrals,"[76] it also acknowledged that "problematic donations involving laboratory companies are [not] solely the result of questionable conduct by laboratory companies."[77] The OIG noted that the conduct of physician recipients and EHR technology vendors was also cause for concern, as commenters reported that vendors encouraged physicians to seek donations from laboratory companies and then charged higher prices for their products because physicians were only paying a fraction of the

---

73. *Id.*
74. 42 C.F.R. § 1001.952(y)(1)(i) (emphasis added).
75. 78 Fed. Reg. at 79,208.
76. *Id.*
77. *Id.* at 79,209.

cost.[78] The exclusion of laboratory companies from the definition of protected EHR donors took effect on March 27, 2014.[79]

When selecting a recipient, the donor cannot directly consider the volume or value of referrals or other business generated between the parties. Notwithstanding the foregoing, the following six selection criteria are deemed to be proper: (1) the size of the recipient's practice; (2) the total number of prescriptions written by the beneficiary; (3) the total number of hours that the beneficiary practices medicine; (4) the recipient's overall use of automated technology; (5) the amount of uncompensated care; or (6) whether the recipient is a member of the donor's medical staff.[80] Thus, in a departure from other safe harbors, a donor can make a donation to a recipient based on the total amount of business received from the physician.

The permissible scope of donated EHR technology is often the most difficult piece of the safe harbor for donors to navigate. Any software, information technology, and training services, including cybersecurity software and services, that are "necessary and used predominantly to create, maintain, transmit, receive, or protect electronic health records" may qualify for protection.[81] Donated software must also be interoperable.[82]

In the 2020 final rule, the OIG also removed a previous requirement that the recipient not already possess equivalent software or

---

78. *See id.*
79. *Id.* at 79,202.
80. 42 C.F.R. § 1001.952(y)(5).
81. *Id.* § 1001.952(y).
82. *Id.* § 1001.952(y)(2). Software is deemed to be interoperable if, on the date the donor provides the software to the recipient, the software has been certified to an edition of EHR certification criteria set forth in applicable federal regulations by a certifying body authorized by the National Coordinator for Health Information Technology. As part of amendments that took effect in January 2021, the OIG removed paragraph (y)(3) from this safe harbor, which prohibited "the donor or any person on the donor's behalf from taking any action to limit or restrict the use, compatibility, or interoperability of the donated EHR items or services." 85 Fed. Reg. at 77,832. The OIG's reasoning for removing paragraph (y)(3) was that the 21st Century Cures Act included language that directly addressed the issue of information blocking better than did paragraph (y)(3). *Id.* Nevertheless, the OIG left an interoperability requirement in paragraph (y)(2) to ensure that "donations of EHR items and services that meet the conditions of this safe harbor further [HHS's] policy goal of an interoperable health system and prevent donations being made with the intent to lock in referrals by limiting the flow of electronic health information." *Id.*

services, recognizing "that there may be valid business or clinical reasons for a recipient to replace an entire system rather than update existing technology" and deciding to treat replacement technology the same as a new donation, so long as all safe harbor requirements are met (e.g., the recipient pay at least 15 percent of the donor's cost for the replacement technology before receiving the items or services).[83]

The "used predominately" requirement of the safe harbor requires that the EHR functions of any donated software must be predominant. In other words, the core functionality of the technology must be the creation, maintenance, transmission, receipt, or protection of individual patients' EHRs. The safe harbor does protect software packages that include other functionality related to the care and treatment of individual patients (e.g., patient administration, scheduling functions, billing, and clinical support), as long as those features are secondary to the EHR function.[84]

2.3.8   Cybersecurity Technology and Related Services

As part of the 2020 final rule, the OIG adopted a new safe harbor to protect the donation of cybersecurity technology and related services in response to the mounting concerns about the financial losses and risks to patients caused by cyberattacks against hospitals and health care providers.[85] This safe harbor is similar in many respects to the EHR donation safe harbor discussed in Subsection 2.3.7.

To qualify for protection under this safe harbor, donors must provide "nonmonetary remuneration" that consists of cybersecurity technology and services.[86] In other words, donors cannot simply compensate or reimburse donation recipients for cybersecurity-related expenditures.

Donations must be documented in a writing that is signed by both parties and that describes, generally, the technology and services

---

83. 85 Fed. Reg. at 77,835.
84. *See id.* at 45,125.
85. 42 C.F.R. § 1001.952(jj).
86. *Id.* § 1001.952(jj).

being provided as well as the amount of the recipient's contribution, if any.

Like the EHR donation safe harbor, the cybersecurity donation safe harbor requires that covered technology and services be "necessary and used predominantly to implement, maintain, or reestablish cybersecurity."[87]

In addition, donors of cybersecurity technology and related services, like EHR donors, cannot directly take into account the volume or value of referrals or other business generated between the parties.[88] Likewise, potential recipients of cybersecurity donations cannot make receipt of a donation, or the amount or nature of the donation, a condition of doing business with the donor.[89]

There are, however, a number of important differences between the EHR and cybersecurity donation safe harbors. First, cybersecurity donors have broader discretion than EHR donors in choosing which technology and services to donate. Whereas the EHR donation safe harbor applies to "nonmonetary remuneration (consisting of items and services in the form of software or information technology and training services, including cybersecurity software and services) necessary and used predominantly to create, maintain, transmit, receive, or protect [EHR]," the cybersecurity donation safe harbor applies to "nonmonetary remuneration (consisting of cybersecurity technology and services) that is necessary and used predominantly to implement, maintain, or reestablish effective cybersecurity." However, while the discretion offered by the cybersecurity donation safe harbor provides flexibility for donors in choosing what to donate, it also creates risk that the donor may donate something that enforcement agencies view as not qualifying for safe harbor protection.

Second, cybersecurity donors may include hardware in a donation. Third, the OIG did not restrict the scope of potential cybersecurity donors. Fourth, recipients of cybersecurity donations are

---

87. *Id.*
88. *Id.* § 1001.952(jj)(1)(i).
89. *Id.* § 1001.952(jj)(2).

not required to pay for any portion of the technology or services they receive.[90]

2.3.9   CMS-Sponsored Model Arrangements and CMS-Sponsored Model Patient Incentives

Effective January 19, 2021, the OIG created a new safe harbor for CMS-sponsored model arrangements and CMS-sponsored model patient incentives that would otherwise rely on the protection of OIG fraud and abuse waivers (see Chapter 3). A CMS-sponsored model is a "model or other initiative being tested or expanded by the [CMS] Innovation Center under section 1115A of the [Social Security] Act or under the Medicare Shared Savings Program under section 1899 of the [Social Security] Act."[91] The OIG's purpose in creating this safe harbor was to largely replace the model-by-model process by which OIG previously approved fraud and abuse waivers for CMS-sponsored payment models. This safe harbor was also designed to provide greater predictability for model participants and uniformity across models.[92] Importantly, the safe harbor is only available for CMS model arrangements for which CMS has determined that the safe harbor is available. As of the date of publication, CMS has started including provisions in payment model participation agreements specifically referencing this safe harbor and CMS's determination that the safe harbor is available for the model participants.

In short, this safe harbor protects (1) exchanges of value between or among parties to an arrangement under a CMS-sponsored model; and (2) CMS-sponsored model patient incentives, for which CMS has determined that this safe harbor is available, assuming all safe harbor conditions are met. For a CMS-sponsored model arrangement, safe harbor requirements include (1) a determination that the model arrangement will advance one or more goals of the CMS-sponsored model; (2) the exchange of value does not induce model parties or other providers or suppliers to furnish medically unnecessary

---

90. *Id.* § 1001.952(jj).
91. 42 C.F.R. § 1001.952(ii)(3)(i)(A).
92. *See* 2020 Final Rule, at 77686.

items or services or reduce or limit medically necessary items or services; (3) parties do not offer, solicit, pay, or receive remuneration to induce or reward federal health care program referrals or other federal health care program business generated outside the model; and (4) the arrangement must be documented in a signed writing that meets certain requirements.[93]

Safe harbor requirements for CMS-sponsored model patient incentives include (1) a determination that the model patient incentive will advance one or more goals of the CMS-sponsored model; (2) the model patient incentive has a direct connection to the patient's health care (unless participation documentation expressly specifies a different standard); and (3) the model patient incentive is furnished by a CMS-sponsored model participant or its agent (unless otherwise specified by the participation documentation).[94]

2.3.10   Value-Based Arrangements

Also effective January 19, 2021, the OIG added three new safe harbors that protect remuneration exchanged between eligible participants in qualifying value-based arrangements. The OIG's primary goal in establishing these safe harbors was to reduce regulatory barriers and advance the health care industry's transition to value-based care. The three value-based safe harbors are broken down by the amount of financial risk assumed under the value-based arrangement. Generally speaking, the more risk that is assumed under an arrangement, the more flexibility that is offered under the applicable safe harbor.

Notably, these safe harbors do not include any fair market value (FMV) requirements. In its final rule, the OIG explained that fraud and abuse concerns that may be addressed by fair market value requirements elsewhere are instead mitigated in the context of the value-based safe harbors by the downside risk-sharing requirements in the substantial downside financial risk and full financial risk safe

---

93. *See* 42 C.F.R. § 1001.952(ii)(1).
94. *See id.* § 1001.952(ii)(1).

harbors, the prohibition on taking into account the volume or value of referrals outside of the target patient population, and other safeguards built into the safe harbors.[95]

2.3.10.1   Relevant Terms

A value-based arrangement is an arrangement entered into between a value-based enterprise (VBE) and one or more of its participants, or among VBE participants in the same VBE, for the provision of one or more value-based activities for a target patient population.[96] A VBE participant is defined as an individual or entity that engages in at least one value-based activity as part of a value-based enterprise, other than a patient acting in their capacity as a patient.[97]

A VBE consists of two or more VBE participants that (1) are collaborating to achieve at least one value-based purpose; (2) are each a party to a value-based arrangement with the other (or at least one other VBE participant in the same VBE); (3) have an accountable body or person responsible for financial and operational oversight of the VBE; and (4) have a governing document describing the VBE and how its participants intend to achieve the VBE's value-based purpose(s).[98] VBEs can vary in size and structure. For example, a VBE could be comprised of a large network of providers and suppliers, or it could be formed by two providers entering into a contractual arrangement to form a value-based arrangement.

A "value-based purpose" means (1) coordinating and managing the care of a target patient population; (2) improving the quality of care for a target patient population; (3) appropriately reducing the costs to, or growth in expenditures of, payors without reducing the quality of care for a target patient population; or (4) transitioning from health care delivery and payment mechanisms based on the volume of items and services provided to mechanisms based on

---

95. 85 Fed. Reg. 77684, 77691 (Dec. 2, 2020).
96. 42 C.F.R. § 1001.952(ee)(14)(vii).
97. *Id.* § 1001.952(ee)(14)(ix).
98. *Id.* § 1001.952(ee)(14)(viii).

the quality of care and control of costs of care for a target patient population.[99]

Notably, the value-based arrangements safe harbors exclude a number of entities from safe harbor protection:

- Pharmaceutical manufacturers
- Distributors
- Wholesalers
- Pharmacy benefit managers
- Laboratory companies
- Pharmacies that primarily compound drugs or dispense compounded drugs
- Manufacturers of devices or medical supplies (except to the extent the entity is a limited technology participant)
- Entities or individuals that sell or rent durable medical equipment, prosthetics, orthotics, and supplies (DMEPOS) (subject to certain exceptions, which exceptions include entities that are limited technology participants)
- Medical device distributors and wholesalers[100]

2.3.10.2 Care Coordination Arrangements to Improve Quality, Health Outcomes, and Efficiency Safe Harbor

The safe harbor for care coordination arrangements to improve quality, health outcomes, and efficiency protects *in-kind* remuneration exchanged between VBE participants that assumes no, or less than substantial, downside financial risk, so long as the remuneration is used predominately to engage in value-based activities directly connected to care coordination for a target patient population.[101] An example of such in-kind remuneration might be a hospital providing to a physician group (1) care managers who ensure that patients receive appropriate care post-discharge and (2) remote

---

99. *Id.* § 1001.952(ee)(14)(x).
100. *Id.* § § 1001.952(ee)(13), (ff)(1), and (gg)(1).
101. *Id.* § 1001.952(ee).

monitoring technology to alert the group when a patient needs intervention to prevent an unnecessary emergency room visit or hospital readmission.

In addition to requiring in-kind remuneration (i.e., not cash), to comply with this safe harbor, the remuneration must (1) be used predominantly to engage in value-based activities directly connected to the care coordination and management of care for the target patient population and not result in more than incidental benefits to persons outside of the target patient population; and (2) not be exchanged or used more than incidentally for the recipients' billing or financial management services or for purposes of marketing items or services furnished by the VBE.

This safe harbor has many additional detailed requirements, including, among others, that (1) the value-based arrangement is commercially reasonable; (2) the terms of the value-based arrangement are set forth in a writing that meets the many requirements articulated in the safe harbor; (3) the VBE participants must establish evidence-based outcome measures against which the recipient of the in-kind remuneration would be measured; (4) the offeror of remuneration must not take into account the volume or value of, or condition the remuneration on, referrals of patients who are not part of the target patient population, or business not covered under the value-based arrangement; (5) recipients must pay at least 15 percent of either the offeror's cost of the remuneration or the fair market value of the remuneration; (6) the value-based arrangement must not limit the VBE participant's ability to make decisions in the best interests of its patients, or direct or restrict referrals to a particular provider, practitioner, or supplier, or induce parties to furnish medically unnecessary items or services or, conversely, to limit medically necessary items or services; and (7) the VBE must monitor, assess, and report to the accountable body or responsible person at least annually any deficiencies in the quality of care and progress toward achieving legitimate outcome or process measures, among others.[102]

---

102. *See id.* § 1001.952(ee).

2.3.10.3 *Value-Based Arrangements with Substantial Downside Financial Risk Safe Harbor*

The value-based arrangements with substantial downside financial risk safe harbor protects payments or anything of value exchanged between a VBE and a VBE participant under a value-based arrangement if certain requirements are met.[103]

To satisfy the requirements of this safe harbor, the VBE must generally have assumed through a written contract or value-based arrangement substantial downside financial risk, which is defined by the safe harbor,[104] from a payor for at least one year, and the VBE participant is at risk for a "meaningful share" (which is also defined by the safe harbor)[105] of the VBE's substantial downside financial risk.

Remuneration provided by or shared among the VBE and VBE participants must be directly connected to at least one of the VBE's value-based purposes and, with limited exceptions, must be used to engage in value-based activities directly connected to the items and services for which the VBE has assumed substantial downside financial risk. Such remuneration may not include the offer or receipt of an ownership or investment interest in an entity or any distributions related to such an interest, and it may not be exchanged or used to market items or services furnished by the VBE or a VBE participant to patients or for patient recruitment activities.

There are a number of similarities between the requirements of this safe harbor and the safe harbor protecting care coordination arrangements. This safe harbor requires that the value-based arrangement be set out in a signed writing specifying all material terms before or contemporaneously with beginning the value-based arrangement and any material changes thereto. The VBE or VBE participant offering remuneration may not take into account the volume or value of, or condition remuneration on, referrals of patients outside of the target patient population or business not covered

---

103. 42 C.F.R. § 1001.952(ff). Importantly, remuneration is not protected if it is exchanged by any of the specifically excluded entities listed previously.
104. *See* 42 C.F.R. § 1001.952(ff)(9)(i).
105. *See id.* § 1001.952(ff)(9)(ii).

by the value-based arrangement. To qualify for protection, a value-based arrangement cannot limit a VBE participant's ability to make decisions in the best interest of its patients, or direct or restrict referrals to a particular provider, practitioner, or supplier in certain circumstances.[106]

Entities wanting to protect their arrangements under this safe harbor will also be subject to record retention requirements outlined in the final rule. VBEs and VBE participants utilizing the safe harbor will need to make compliance-related records available to HHS for at least six years.[107]

2.3.10.4 *Value-Based Arrangements with Full Financial Risk Safe Harbor*

Similar to the safe harbor for value-based arrangements with substantial downside financial risk, the safe harbor for value-based arrangements with full financial risk protects monetary or in-kind remuneration from a VBE to a VBE participant and requires that the arrangement be documented in a writing that meets certain conditions.[108] This safe harbor likewise prohibits the reduction or limitation of medically necessary items or services, as well as the taking into account or conditioning of remuneration on referrals of patients who are not part of the target population and business not covered by the arrangement, among other overlapping requirements.

However, unlike the other safe harbors for value-based arrangements, this safe harbor requires that the VBE assume full financial responsibility for the costs of all items and services covered by a payor for each patient in the target population for a term of one year and that the remuneration at issue be paid prospectively.[109] This safe harbor also requires that the VBE provide or arrange for a quality assurance program for services furnished to the target patient population that includes certain elements. Of all the safe harbors for

---

106. *See id.* §§ 1001.952(ff)(5), (6), (7).
107. *See id.* § 1001.952(ff)(8).
108. 42 C.F.R. § 1001.952(gg).
109. *See id.* § 1001.952(gg)(2).

value-based arrangements, this safe harbor is designed to afford the most flexibility to the parties, but given the level of risk it requires the parties to assume, this provision may ultimately prove to be of limited utility to parties considering a value-based arrangement.

Fraud and Abuse Waivers

3

Even though the federal fraud and abuse laws, including the Anti-Kickback Statute (AKS), are intended to protect the integrity of the health care system, at times they stand in the way of innovation in the health care sector.[1] In an effort to address this obstacle to health care reform, Centers for Medicare and Medicaid Services (CMS) and the Office of Inspector General (OIG) have allowed waivers of certain federal fraud and abuse laws for several CMS payment and care delivery models, such as the Medicare Shared Savings Program (MSSP), the Bundled Payment for Care Improvement (BPCI), the Comprehensive Care for Joint Replacement Model, the Direct Contracting Model, and the Kidney Care Choices Model.[2] The waivers are all model-specific, vary somewhat among the models, and include a number of required conditions. But, typically, the waivers waive the AKS, the Stark Law, and the provision of the Civil Monetary Penalties Law (CMPL) that prohibits beneficiary inducement (Beneficiary Inducement CMPL) with respect to arrangements between the Accountable

---

1. *See* U.S. Gov't Accountability Office, GAO-12-355, Implementation of Financial Incentive Programs under Federal Fraud and Abuse Laws (Mar. 30, 2012), http://www.gao.gov/products/GAO-12-355.
2. *See* Fraud and Abuse Waivers for Select CMS Models and Programs, https://www.cms.gov/medicare/physician-self-referral/fraud-and-abuse-waivers.

Care Organization (ACO) and participating providers and suppliers; shared savings distributions; and items or services provided by the ACO or its providers and suppliers to beneficiaries for free or below fair market value. Following is an example of some of the most frequently utilized waivers—the MSSP fraud and abuse waivers.

3.1 The MSSP Fraud and Abuse Waivers

The MSSP is one of the cornerstones of the efforts of the Affordable Care Act (ACA) to encourage the health care system to implement more cost-effective approaches to providing high-quality care. CMS established the MSSP to enhance coordination and cooperation among providers with the goal of improving the quality of care that Medicare fee-for-service (FFS) beneficiaries receive while at the same time reducing costs. To participate in the MSSP, eligible providers, hospitals, and suppliers may participate in or create an ACO.[3] The MSSP promotes accountability for the care of Medicare FFS beneficiaries, requires coordination of care for all services provided to them, and encourages investment in infrastructure and the redesign of the care process.[4] ACOs that meet MSSP performance standards may receive additional Medicare payments (i.e., a share of the savings they generate).[5]

---

3. Ctrs. for Medicare & Medicaid Servs., Shared Savings Program, http://www.cms.gov/Medicare/Medicare-Fee-for-Service-Payment/sharedsavingsprogram/index.html.
4. *Id.*
5. *See* Thomas S. Crane, Brian P. Dunphy & Karen S. Lovitch, *Delicate Balance: Waiver of Fraud and Abuse Laws and Implementation of Program Integrity Requirements for the Medicare Shared Savings Program*, Health Care Fraud Rep. (BNA) (Nov. 30, 2011), https://www.bloomberglaw.com/product/blaw/bloomberglawnews/health-law-and-business/X8URKIDO000000?bc=W1siU2VhcmNoICYgQnJvd3NlIiwiaHR0cHM6Ly93d3cuYmxvb2 2liZXJnbGF3LmNvbS9wcm9kdWN0L2JsYXcvYmxvb21lcmdsYXduZXdzL3Jlc3VsdHMvOTBiZmVkNmE1NjU zODJlYWRjNDQyNjMxNTJhN2 zODJIYWRjNDQyNjMxNTJhN2 zODJlYWRjNDQyNjMxNTJhN2 zODJlWRjNDQyNjMxNTJhNzFmMGEiXV0=2c9918d8dd113da126d4e59fefed08e1b5bfccfc&bna_news_filter=health-law-and-business&criteria_id=90bfed6a565382eadc44263152a71f0a&search32=l1K72sUSFMyy7ERayLdq6w%3D%3DU2RBWnMlkdAkJz03TbotlPO-wHB4RWLTPJQjuAoFgDVtMk_e68wkvPbrFLCCJpcLZ-j0nCibG-SYLV8raYfXoUHgASXULRBM9d3KkJT2ch9c0RtJNRXgKoL-qRhAUPr3vEo2xSehx8Z6E1nPrffl1xFih_Ad5tebp7MGZAjSp93opk_9Mc3kuOl_0YcX_LYHez6SybwW_uTWM-9C7lJJKidJYFxA1DM7cvyYlv6TgVdRH_FLw6b8qUg1F8v1zTAsS8qHpIj0FWPH36_ihzSqeqQqBgvmru0WAUSU1Vtp6BaA6QOtLPycm7-Ky4BHd0Dc0JOwE8IfMn0wfYAl_OBE4iBpSDR6i3PFQCSxbxnvGCxBUDRFozENn-Hx15Q5XOG.

Technically, the shared savings and other aspects of an ACO's arrangements could implicate many laws that address overutilization, underutilization, waste, and health care decision-making skewed by financial incentives, including the AKS. To facilitate the development of ACOs, CMS and the OIG issued a 2011 interim final rule and 2015 final rule (the Waiver Rule) detailing the circumstances in which the agencies would waive certain health care fraud and abuse laws in connection with the MSSP.[6] Through the Waiver Rule, Congress authorized five waivers that apply to certain fraud and abuse laws, including the AKS, the Stark Law, and the provision of the Civil Monetary Penalties Law (CMPL) that prohibits beneficiary inducement (Beneficiary Inducement CMPL). The waivers may be briefly summarized as follows:

- *The Shared Savings Distribution Waiver.* This waiver of the Stark Law and the AKS applies to distributions and uses of payments earned under the MSSP.
- *The Compliance with Physician Self-Referral Law Waiver.* This waiver of the AKS covers ACO arrangements that implicate the Stark Law but meet an existing Stark Law exception.
- *The ACO Preparticipation Waiver.* This waiver protects certain start-up arrangements that precede an ACO's participation agreement (provided certain conditions are met). It applies to the Stark Law and the AKS. The Waiver Rule includes a long list of the kinds of activities that would reasonably qualify as start-up arrangements, indicating that CMS and the OIG understand the breadth of activities necessary to start an ACO. However, this waiver excludes home health suppliers and pharmaceutical and device manufacturers due to program integrity and other concerns.
- *The ACO Participation Waiver.* This waiver extends to the Stark Law and the AKS and protects most aspects of the ACO's ongoing

---

6. Medicare Program; Final Waivers in Connection with the Medicare Shared Savings Program, 76 Fed. Reg. 67,992 (Nov. 2, 2011); 80 Fed. Reg. 66,726 (Oct. 29, 2015).

operations from the start date of the ACO's participation agreement until the earlier of six months after expiration or the ACO's voluntary termination of its participation agreement. If for some reason CMS terminates the ACO's participation agreement, the waiver period ends on the date of the termination notice.

- *The Patient Incentive Waiver.* This waiver was designed to encourage patients to be engaged in the management of their own care, including participation in preventive care and compliance with treatment regimes. As such, CMS and OIG established a waiver of the Beneficiary Inducement CMPL and the AKS to allow an ACO and its participants and providers/suppliers to provide items or services to beneficiaries for free or below fair market value (in certain circumstances).

While parties seeking to take advantage of these waivers do not need to notify or seek approval from CMS, certain of these waivers, including the ACO Preparticipation and Participation Waivers, must meet certain documentation and disclosure requirements. These two waivers require the ACO to authorize the arrangement as being reasonably related to the purposes of the MSSP and to document its authorization contemporaneous with the establishment of the arrangement. In addition, the description of the arrangement must be publicly disclosed.

3.2 Transition from Model-by-Model Waivers to Broadly Applicable Safe Harbors

As discussed in Subsection 2.3.9, new safe harbors for CMS-sponsored model arrangements and CMS-sponsored model patient incentives took effect in January 2021 that otherwise would have required the protection of specific, model-by-model fraud and abuse waivers, similar to those that apply to the MSSP.[7]

A CMS-sponsored model is a "model or other initiative being tested or expanded by the [CMS] Innovation Center under section

---

7. 42 C.F.R. § 1001.952(ii).

1115A of the [Social Security] Act or under the Medicare Shared Savings Program under section 1899 of the [Social Security] Act."[8] Examples include the Bundled Payments for Care Improvement Advanced Model and the Global and Professional Options of the Direct Contracting Model. The OIG indicated that it expected this new approach would provide greater predictability for model participants and uniformity across models.[9]

Importantly, the safe harbor only protects arrangements for which CMS has determined that the safe harbor is available. Initially there was some confusion on whether and how CMS was going to make such determinations, and whether the safe harbor would be available for certain payment models. However, CMS recently started including provisions in payment model participation agreements specifically referencing this safe harbor and its determination that the safe harbor is available for the model participants.

---

8. *See* 2020 Final Rule, at 77809; 42 C.F.R. § 1001.952(ii)(3).
9. *See* 2020 Final Rule, at 77686.

Sources of Guidance

4

Given that a violation of the Anti-Kickback Statute (AKS) can have serious consequences, it is important to consult the various sources of guidance before proceeding with an arrangement that could implicate the statute. When the Office of Inspector General (OIG) for the U.S. Department of Health and Human Services (HHS) announces new safe harbors, or makes changes to existing safe harbors, it typically provides some insight into its interpretation of those safe harbors in the preambles to the rules published in the *Federal Register*. From time to time, the OIG also publishes fraud alerts, special advisory bulletins, and other guidance documents of general applicability as well as advisory opinions. Although advisory opinions are binding only on the requesting parties, they nevertheless provide a glimpse into how the OIG views various types of business arrangements. Finally, the courts have decided a number of cases that speak to the application of the AKS.[1]

---

1. During the COVID-19 national public health emergency, the OIG announced that it would relax enforcement of certain of its administrative enforcement authorities, including the AKS, as applied to arrangements directly connected to the public health emergency in circumstances where the OIG determined that doing so would allow health care providers sufficient regulatory flexibility to appropriately respond to COVID-19 concerns and likewise advance the health care industry's provision of patient care and services related to the COVID-19 pandemic. The OIG conveyed its decisions in this

4.1 Preambles to Proposed, Interim, and Final Rules

The preambles to the proposed, interim, and final rules published by the OIG provide invaluable insight into how the OIG might interpret and apply the AKS and its statutory exceptions and regulatory safe harbors.

The Medicare and Medicaid Patient and Program Protection Act of 1987 required, in part, that the OIG promulgate safe harbors to identify practices or arrangements permitted under the AKS.[2] Since 1989, the OIG has published a number of proposed rules, interim final rules, and final rules in the *Federal Register*. The proposed rules and some interim final rules introduced proposed safe harbor provisions and allowed the public the opportunity to submit comments to the OIG. In the interim final rules, the OIG also responded to certain comments, questions, or requests it received in response to a proposed rule and explained the reasons for its responses. In the final rules, the OIG set forth the version of a given safe harbor that would be codified in the *Code of Federal Regulations* applicable to the AKS (42 C.F.R. § 1001.952) and again explained its decisions.

The OIG's rules published to date implementing the AKS are shown in Table 1.

Table 1. Proposed, Interim, and Final AKS Rules

Rule	Date of Publication	Citation	Description
Proposed Rule	January 23, 1989	54 Fed. Reg. 3088	Proposed original ten safe harbors.
Final Rule	July 29, 1991	56 Fed. Reg. 35,952	Promulgated original ten safe harbors.
Interim Final Rule	November 5, 1992	57 Fed. Reg. 52,723	Set forth three new safe harbors addressing managed care plans.

area by responding to a series of Frequently Asked Questions. The OIG published these responses on its website (https://oig.hhs.gov/coronavirus/authorities-faq.asp).
2. Pub. L. No. 100-93, § 14, 101 Stat. 680 (1987).

Rule	Date of Publication	Citation	Description
Proposed Rule	September 21, 1993	58 Fed. Reg. 49,008	Set forth seven additional safe harbors.
Proposed Rule	July 21, 1994	59 Fed. Reg. 37,202	Proposed clarifications to the original safe harbors published in the July 29, 1991, final rule.
Final Rule	January 25, 1996	61 Fed. Reg. 2122	Revised the November 5, 1992, final rule setting forth three managed care safe harbors.
Interim Final Rule	November 19, 1999	64 Fed. Reg. 63,504	Addressed federal health care programs, fraud and abuse, and a statutory exception to the AKS for shared risk arrangements.
Final Rule	November 19, 1999	64 Fed. Reg. 63,518	Clarified the initial safe harbors and established additional safe harbors.
Proposed Rule	May 22, 2000	65 Fed. Reg. 32,060	Proposed the ambulance restocking safe harbor.
Final Rule	December 4, 2001	66 Fed. Reg. 62,979	Finalized the ambulance restocking safe harbor.
Proposed Rule	September 25, 2002	67 Fed. Reg. 60,202	Proposed a safe harbor for the waiver of Medicare SELECT beneficiary coinsurance and deductible amounts.
Proposed Rule	July 1, 2005	70 Fed. Reg. 38,081	Proposed a safe harbor for certain federally qualified health center arrangements.
Proposed Rule	October 11, 2005	70 Fed. Reg. 59,015	Proposed a safe harbor for certain electronic prescribing technology donation arrangements.
Final Rule	August 8, 2006	71 Fed. Reg. 45,110	Finalized the safe harbor for certain electronic prescribing and electronic health records technology donations.
Final Rule	October 4, 2007	72 Fed. Reg. 56,632	Finalized the safe harbor for certain federally qualified health center arrangements.

Rule	Date of Publication	Citation	Description
Proposed Rule	April 10, 2013	78 Fed. Reg. 21,314	Sought comments on amendments to the safe harbor for electronic health records donations.
Final Rule	December 27, 2013	78 Fed. Reg. 79,202	Amended the safe harbor for electronic health records technology donations.
Proposed Rule	October 3, 2014	79 Fed. Reg. 59,717	Proposed to amend the referral service safe harbor and to add five new safe harbors for various beneficiary discounts and cost-sharing programs and for certain federally qualified health center arrangements.
Final Rule	December 7, 2016	81 Fed. Reg. 88,368	Modified existing safe harbors to include technical corrections and finalized new safe harbors designed to protect various beneficiary discounts and cost-sharing programs.
Proposed Rule	February 6, 2019	84 Fed. Reg. 2,340	Proposed to amend the discount safe harbor and to create two new safe harbors, one of which would protect certain point-of-sale reductions in price on prescription pharmaceutical products and the second of which would protect certain pharmacy benefit manager service fees.

Rule	Date of Publication	Citation	Description
Proposed Rule	October 17, 2019	84 Fed. Reg. 55,694	Proposed to add safe harbor protections for certain coordinated care and associated value-based arrangements, for certain patient engagement and support arrangements, for donations of cybersecurity technology, and for beneficiary incentives under the Medicare Shared Savings Program. Proposed to amend existing safe harbor provisions protecting certain electronic health record technology donations, warranties, local transportation, and personal services and management contracts.
Final Rule	November 30, 2020	85 Fed. Reg. 76,666	Finalized amendments to the discount safe harbor and the creation of two new safe harbors for certain point-of-sales price reductions on prescription pharmaceutical products and for certain pharmacy benefit manager service fees. The effective date of these amendments has been delayed until January 1, 2026.

Rule	Date of Publication	Citation	Description
Final Rule	December 2, 2020	85 Fed. Reg. 77,684	Finalized six new safe harbors protecting certain value-based arrangements; patient engagement tools and supports furnished to participants in a value-based enterprise; CMS-sponsored model arrangements and patient incentives that would otherwise require OIG fraud and abuse waivers; and the provision of cybersecurity technology and services. Also finalized modifications to existing safe harbors for electronic health records technology donations, personal services and management contracts, warranties, and local transportation.

4.2 Advisory Opinions

In 1996, Congress enacted legislation requiring the OIG to issue advisory opinions on whether a business arrangement or activity would run afoul of the AKS and other authorities within the OIG's jurisdiction, such as the Civil Monetary Penalties Law.[3] Since 1997, the OIG has regularly issued advisory opinions to one or more requesting parties on the application of the AKS and certain other fraud and abuse laws to existing or proposed arrangements. OIG advisory opinions are case specific and legally binding only on the OIG and the requesting parties. However, these opinions provide insight to the public about how the OIG views certain conduct under the AKS, including (1) what the OIG considers remuneration, (2) whether certain arrangements meet statutory exception or safe harbor require-

---

3. *See* 42 U.S.C. § 1320a-7d(b); *see also* 42 C.F.R. pt. 1008.

ments, and (3) whether the OIG would impose sanctions, even if the AKS is implicated. The OIG will not opine on fair market value.

4.3 Fraud Alerts, Special Advisory Bulletins, and Other Guidance

On the one hand, safe harbor regulations are intended to describe arrangements that do not violate the AKS. On the other hand, the OIG also identifies, through the issuance of special fraud alerts, special advisory bulletins, and other guidance, certain practices or arrangements that are subject to scrutiny under the AKS.

Since 1989, the OIG has issued more than a dozen special fraud alerts regarding the application of the AKS to various arrangements. The special fraud alerts have addressed the OIG's position on, among other things, (1) joint venture relationships, (2) arrangements for the provision of clinical laboratory services, (3) prescription drug marketing practices, (4) hospital incentives to referring physicians, (5) routine waiver of Part B copayments and deductibles, (6) home health fraud, (7) various arrangements with nursing homes, (8) rental of space in physician offices by persons or entities to which physicians refer, (9) arrangements with physician-owned entities, (10) payments by laboratories to referring physicians, and (11) speaker programs.[4]

Additionally, the OIG has issued special advisory bulletins on a variety of topics, including (1) the offer of gifts and inducements to beneficiaries, (2) contractual joint ventures, (3) business consultant practices, (4) hospital-physician incentive plans for Medicare and Medicaid beneficiaries enrolled in managed care plans, and (5) hospital payments to physicians to reduce or limit services to beneficiaries.[5]

---

4. A complete list of and links to the OIG special fraud alerts are available at http://oig .hhs.gov/compliance/alerts/index.asp.
5. A complete list of and links to the OIG special advisory bulletins is available at http:// oig.hhs.gov/compliance/alerts/bulletins/index.asp.

The OIG has also published responses to various compliance inquiries, including requests for guidance regarding (1) the provision of free computers, fax machines, and other goods to physicians; (2) the provision of free goods and services by various health care providers (e.g., clinical laboratories); (3) discount arrangements involving clinical laboratories, skilled nursing facilities, ambulance companies, and hospitals; (4) waiver of beneficiary cost-sharing amounts; (5) the application of the AKS to the acquisition of physician practices; (6) joint venture arrangements; (7) up-front rebates, prebates, and signing bonus payments; (8) physician investments in medical device manufacturers and distributors; (9) physician compensation arrangements; and (10) gifts of nominal value to Medicare and Medicaid beneficiaries.[6]

Finally, the OIG occasionally issues letters to health care providers alerting them to OIG policies and processes, inviting providers to engage in the OIG's antifraud initiatives, and providing updates related to ongoing projects to fight fraud, waste, and abuse in federal health care programs.[7]

4.4 OIG Compliance Guidance

Starting in the mid to late 1990s, the OIG began promoting the adoption of corporate compliance programs by issuing compliance guidance documents for various health care industry segments, including clinical laboratories; hospitals; home health agencies; third-party medical billing companies; companies selling durable medical equipment, prosthetics, orthotics, and supplies; hospices; Medicare+Choice (now known as Medicare Advantage) organizations;

---

6. A complete list of and links to these guidance documents is available at http://oig.hhs.gov/compliance/alerts/guidance/index.asp.
7. A complete list of and links to the open letters is available at http://oig.hhs.gov/compliance/open-letters/index.asp.

nursing facilities; individual and small group physician practices; ambulance suppliers; and pharmaceutical manufacturers.[8]

The guidance documents identify those segments of the health care industry that the OIG considers to be at "high risk" for fraud and abuse. The purpose of the compliance program guidance is to encourage these high-risk segments of the health care industry to establish compliance programs that include various internal controls to ensure and monitor adherence to applicable statutes, regulations, and program requirements.

The compliance program guidance documents also identify specific risk areas for the entities to which the guidance is directed and make recommendations for how these risk areas can be managed in order to avoid implicating the AKS.

4.5 Examples of Enforcement Actions

As written, the AKS could apply to a broad array of conduct and arrangements, but over time, the federal agencies tasked with enforcing the statute have demonstrated some trends in their areas of focus. These enforcement trends, and related settlements and litigation, provide helpful insight into how the AKS is utilized and interpreted in practice. Some examples of areas where the federal government has focused with respect to AKS enforcement include (1) arrangements involving the provision of cash and items of value to providers, (2) the use of foundations as conduits for pharmaceutical manufacturers to cover patient cost-sharing amounts, and (3) payments by Electronic Health Records (EHR) vendors to providers to incentivize the providers to use the vendors' EHR software.

---

8. A complete list of and links to the OIG compliance guidance documents is available at https://oig.hhs.gov/compliance/compliance-guidance/index.asp.

4.5.1 Provision of Cash and Items of Value to Providers

For many years, the federal government has focused its enforcement efforts on alleged AKS violations involving the provision of cash and items of value to providers. The government often pursues such actions under the federal False Claims Act (FCA), but the FCA violations at issue result from claims arguably tainted by underlying AKS violations. For example, in cases where cash and items of value are given to health care providers with intent to induce those providers to prescribe a manufacturer's products or a laboratory's services in violation of the AKS, claims submitted to federal health care programs for those products or services are arguably tainted by an AKS violation and thus false for purposes of the FCA (see Chapter 5). One well-known example of AKS enforcement involving payments made to physicians involved several laboratory companies (among other defendants) that were prosecuted in connection with an alleged kickback scheme that included, among other remuneration, payments to physicians to cover the costs of "processing and handling fees" associated with collection and shipping of patient specimens.[9] The government alleged that such payments were kickbacks to the providers in return for test orders that were disguised as "processing and handling fees" (the government also alleged that these payments exceeded fair market value).[10]

An example of AKS enforcement actions involving the provision of items of value to referral sources includes speaker programs where, for example, drug and device manufacturers invite referral sources to a speaker program hosted at a restaurant. In many such cases, the government has argued that while the purported purpose of

---

9. *See, e.g.*, United States, et al. ex rel. Lutz, et al. v. Health Diagnostic Laboratory, Inc., et al., Case No. 9:14-CV-0230-RMG (D.S.C.); and United States ex rel. Riedel v. Health Diagnostic Laboratory, Inc., et al., Case No. 1:11-CV-02308 (D.D.C.).

10. *See, e.g.*, United States ex rel. Riedel v. Health Diagnostic Laboratory, Inc., et al., Case No. 1:11-CV-02308 (D.D.C.). *See also* DOJ Press Release, U.S. Obtains $114 Million Judgment Against Three Individuals for Paying Kickbacks for Laboratory Referrals and Causing Claims for Medically Unnecessary Tests (May 29, 2018), https://www.justice.gov/usao-dc/pr/us-obtains-114-million-judgment-against-three-individuals-paying-kickbacks-laboratory.

the speaker program was to educate potential referrers on topics relevant to the program sponsor's products and that the meal provided was incidental to the presentation, the actual presentations had minimal educational value and the real purpose of the program was to provide potential referrers with lavish meals and alcohol (i.e., items of value).[11] The government has also taken issue with fees paid to providers who speak at these programs, arguing that such payments were disguised kickbacks because the presentations the providers were paid to give had little educational value and really served as a vehicle to compensate physicians for referrals to the company.[12] In November 2020, OIG issued a Special Fraud Alert cautioning of the risks inherent to speaker programs.[13]

4.5.2 Patient Assistance Programs

Over the past several years, another area of focus for FCA enforcement predicated on alleged AKS violations has been patient assistance programs (PAPs). PAPs are typically offered by pharmaceutical manufacturers (and others) to assist patients with their portion of the cost for prescription drugs covered by federal health care programs (e.g., Medicare).

PAPs are structured and operated in many different ways. For example, PAPs may offer to patients cash subsidies, free or reduced price drugs, or both. Some PAPs are affiliated with particular pharmaceutical manufacturers; others are operated by independent

---

11. *See, e.g.*, DOJ Press Release, Shire PLC Subsidiaries to Pay $350 Million to Settle False Claims Act Allegations (Jan. 11, 2017); DOJ Press Release, Opioid Manufacturer Insys Therapeutics Agrees to Enter $225 Million Global Resolution of Criminal and Civil Investigations (June 5, 2019); DOJ Press Release, Acting Manhattan U.S. Attorney Announces $678 Million Settlement of Fraud Lawsuit against Novartis Pharmaceuticals for Operating Sham Speaker Programs through Which It Paid over $100 Million to Doctors to Unlawfully Induce Them to Prescribe Novartis Drugs (July 1, 2020).

12. *See, e.g.*, DOJ Press Release, Shire PLC Subsidiaries to Pay $350 Million to Settle False Claims Act Allegations (Jan. 11, 2017); DOJ Press Release, Opioid Manufacturer Insys Therapeutics Agrees to Enter $225 Million Global Resolution of Criminal and Civil Investigations (June 5, 2019); DOJ Press Release, Acting Manhattan U.S. Attorney Announces $678 Million Settlement of Fraud Lawsuit against Novartis Pharmaceuticals for Operating Sham Speaker Programs through Which It Paid over $100 Million to Doctors to Unlawfully Induce Them to Prescribe Novartis Drugs (July 1, 2020).

13. *See* OIG Special Fraud Alert: Speaker Programs, November 16, 2020.

charitable organizations (such as, for example, patient advocacy and support organizations).

PAPs may offer assistance directly to patients whose drugs are not covered by an insurance program or they may assist insured patients by covering the cost of some or all of the patients' copayments, coinsurance amounts, or deductibles, referred to generally as the "patient responsibility amount." Assigning patient responsibility amounts to the cost of drugs is referred to as "cost-sharing" and is intended to serve as a check on health care costs. If a drug is extremely expensive, the patient's responsibility amount will be proportionally expensive.

In 2005, the OIG issued a Special Advisory Bulletin addressing the use of PAPs to assist financially needy Medicare Part D beneficiaries with patient responsibility amounts and whether those arrangements implicated the AKS.[14] The OIG advised that subsidies provided by PAPs operated by pharmaceutical manufacturers "would be squarely prohibited by the [AKS], because the manufacturer would be giving something of value (i.e., the subsidy) to beneficiaries to use its product," but added that "pharmaceutical manufacturers can donate to *bona fide* independent charity PAPs," provided that certain safeguards exist: (1) neither the pharmaceutical manufacturer nor any of its affiliates may directly or indirectly influence or control the charity or the subsidy program; (2) the assistance provided to the patient cannot be attributed to the donating manufacturer; (3) the assistance must be provided without regard to the manufacturer's interests or the beneficiary's choice of product, provider, practitioner, supplier, or Medicare Part D drug plan; (4) the charity must provide assistance "based upon a reasonable, verifiable, and uniform measure of financial need that is applied in a consistent manner"; and (5) the manufacturer cannot solicit or receive data from the charity that would facilitate the manufacturer in correlating its donations to prescriptions for its product.[15]

---

14. *See* 70 Fed. Reg. 70623 (Nov. 22, 2005).
15. *Id.* at 70626.

Beginning in 2017, the Department of Justice (DOJ) announced the first in a series of FCA settlements predicated on alleged AKS violations involving pharmaceutical manufacturer conduct that the OIG explicitly advised against in its 2005 OIG Special Advisory Bulletin.[16] For example, the government alleged that certain manufacturers were purporting to donate to independent, charitable foundation PAPs, when in reality the foundations were not independent, and acted as conduits to cover patient responsibility amounts specifically for the manufacturer's drugs. Manufacturers were also accused of tracking their donations to ensure that they achieved the purpose of covering the manufacturer's drug.[17] This conduct, the government alleged, allowed the manufacturers to drive up the cost of their drugs and shift the expense to the Medicare program funded by American taxpayers. The cost-shifting problem was compounded because prescribers were not deterred from prescribing expensive drugs to patients by high patient cost-sharing amounts, as these payments were covered by the PAPs instead of the patients. Notably, although the government did not say so explicitly, the AKS theory underlying some part of these settlements appears to be that manufacturers provided remuneration *to beneficiaries* by covering patient responsibility amounts.[18]

4.5.3 Electronic Health Records Donations

Donations of EHR software to health care providers have also been the subject of enforcement actions in recent years. As discussed in

---

16. *See, e.g.*, DOJ Press Release, Novartis Agrees to Pay Over $51 Million to Resolve Allegations that It Paid Kickbacks through Co-Pay Foundations (July 1, 2020); DOJ Press Release, United States Files False Claims Act Complaint against Drug Maker Teva Pharmaceuticals Alleging Illegal Kickbacks (Aug. 18, 2020); DOJ Press Release, Gilead Agrees to Pay $97 Million to Resolve Alleged False Claims Act Liability for Paying Kickbacks (Sept. 23, 2020).
17. DOJ Press Release, Novartis Agrees to Pay over $51 Million to Resolve Allegations that It Paid Kickbacks through Co-Pay Foundations (July 1, 2020); DOJ Press Release, Gilead Agrees to Pay $97 Million to Resolve Alleged False Claims Act Liability for Paying Kickbacks (Sept. 23, 2020).
18. *See, e.g.*, DOJ Press Release, Novartis Agrees to Pay over $51 Million to Resolve Allegations that It Paid Kickbacks through Co-Pay Foundations (July 1, 2020); DOJ Press Release, United States Files False Claims Act Complaint against Drug Maker Teva Pharmaceuticals Alleging Illegal Kickbacks (Aug. 18, 2020); DOJ Press Release, Gilead Agrees to Pay $97 Million to Resolve Alleged False Claims Act Liability for Paying Kickbacks (Sept. 23, 2020).

Subsection 2.3.7, in 2006, the OIG adopted a safe harbor to permit the donation of EHR software and services to physician practices, among other recipients. In recent years, enforcement agencies have pursued (and settled) several matters involving allegations that EHR vendors were offering improper remuneration to existing customers that violated the AKS and thus the FCA.[19] For example, EHR vendors have been accused of operating marketing referral programs that included cash bonuses and percentage success payments to existing customers in return for those customers' recommending the vendor's EHR products to prospective clients.[20] Other vendors have been accused of paying provider-clients for successful referrals of another provider-client, providing remuneration in the form of entertainment to prospective and current customers, making cash payments for lead generation, and paying competing companies exiting the EHR market that successfully converted their customers into customers of the EHR vendor.[21] In these cases, the vendors were accused of providing illegal remuneration in the form of cash or items of value, but what the government has not explicitly articulated (in publicly available documents) is how this remuneration was paid *to induce referrals of items or services that were reimbursable by federal health care programs*, as required by the AKS. In a subset of cases, certain EHR donation recipients submitted certifications to the federal government in return for incentive payments offered by CMS related to use of certain technology, but where the donation recipient was not submitting such certifications, the nexus between the alleged remuneration and claims to federal health care programs is less clear.

---

19. *See* DOJ Press Release, Miami-Based CareCloud Health, Inc. Agrees to Pay $3.8 Million to Resolve Allegations that It Paid Illegal Kickbacks (Apr. 30, 2021); DOJ Press Release, Athenahealth Agrees to Pay $18.25 Million to Resolve Allegations that It Paid Illegal Kickbacks (Jan. 28, 2021); DOJ Press Release, Electronic Health Records Vendor to Pay $155 Million to Settle False Claims Act Allegations (May 31, 2017).
20. *See* DOJ Press Release, Miami-Based CareCloud Health, Inc. Agrees to Pay $3.8 Million to Resolve Allegations that it Paid Illegal Kickbacks (Apr. 30, 2021).
21. *See* DOJ Press Release, Athenahealth Agrees to Pay $18.25 Million to Resolve Allegations that It Paid Illegal Kickbacks (Jan. 28, 2021).

Related Statutes

5

Business arrangements and practices that potentially violate the Anti-Kickback Statute (AKS) also may implicate other laws intended to combat health care fraud and abuse. This chapter examines those statutes that arise most often in government investigations and litigation involving the AKS.

5.1 The Federal False Claims Act

Because the AKS does not offer a private right of action, private parties often pursue alleged AKS violations under the federal False Claims Act (FCA), which allows anyone who is an "original source" (often referred to as a "whistleblower" or a "relator") to bring suit on behalf of the government and to share in the financial recoveries. In short, the FCA provides that any person who

- knowingly presents, or causes to be presented, a false or fraudulent claim for payment or approval to the federal government, or
- knowingly makes, uses, or causes to be made or used, a false record or statement material to a false or fraudulent claim to the federal government,

is liable for a civil penalty of not less than $11,665 and not more than $23,331,[1] plus three times the amount of damages that the government sustains.[2] The simple example shown in Table 1 highlights the gravity of these penalties.

Table 1. Example of FCA Penalties

	Claims Filed	Dollars per Claim	Reimbursement	Potential FCA Liability
FCA Violation	1,000 claims submitted	$100 per claim	1,000 claims × $100/claim = $100,000 in reimbursement	1,000 claims × $23,331/claim = $23.33 million (potential penalties) *plus* $100,000 × 3 = $300,000 (treble damages) = $23,633,000 total potential liability.

The Department of Justice (DOJ) has recovered more than $64 billion under the FCA since 1986, when the FCA was amended to increase incentives for private citizens to file suit under the FCA on behalf of the government, which is discussed in more detail later in the chapter.[3] Since 2009, DOJ's recoveries in health care fraud settlements and judgments have exceeded $2 billion per year.[4] Of

---

1. 31 U.S.C. § 3729(a)(1)(G) provides that the civil penalties assessed under the FCA may be adjusted by the Federal Civil Penalties Inflation Adjustment Act of 1990 (Pub. L. No. 101-410, 104 Stat. 890 (codified at 28 U.S.C. § 2461)). *See also* 28 C.F.R. § 85.3(a)(9). The civil monetary penalties amount for violations of the FCA assessed after June 19, 2020, whose associated violations occurred after November 2, 2015, is currently set at a minimum of $11,665 and a maximum of $23,331 per "false" claim submitted. 28 C.F.R. § 85.5.
2. 31 U.S.C. § 3729(a). The terms "knowing" and "knowingly" mean that a person (1) has actual knowledge of the information; (2) acts in deliberate ignorance of the truth or falsity of the information; or (3) acts in reckless disregard of the truth or falsity of the information. Proof of specific intent to defraud is not required. *Id.* § 3729(b)(1).
3. Press Release, U.S. Dep't of Justice, Justice Department Recovers $2.2 Billion from False Claims Act Cases in Fiscal Year 2020 (Jan. 14, 2021), https://www.justice.gov/opa/pr/justice-department-recovers-over-22-billion-false-claims-act-cases-fiscal-year-2020.
4. Press Release, U.S. Dep't of Justice, Justice Department Recovers $2.2 Billion from False Claims Act Cases in Fiscal Year 2019 (Jan. 9, 2020), https://www.justice.gov/opa/pr/justice-department-recovers-over-3-billion-false-claims-act-cases-fiscal-year-2019.

the $2.2 billion recovered in fiscal year (FY) 2020, $1.8 billion was recovered in health care fraud cases.[5] In FY 2020 alone, relators filed 672 qui tam actions, and were awarded a total of $309 million.[6]

Since enactment of the Affordable Care Act (ACA) in 2010, the AKS has explicitly stated that claims for items or services resulting from an AKS violation are false or fraudulent for purposes of the FCA.[7] An FCA action thus can be based on an allegation that the defendant knowingly submitted (or caused to be submitted) to the government claims for items or services that were tainted by an underlying AKS violation. Prior to enactment of the ACA, much litigation focused on whether alleged violations of the AKS could give rise to FCA liability. This theory of falsity was predicated on the argument that the defendant knowingly submitted (or caused the submission of) "tainted" claims by violating the AKS in the course of providing the services, and compliance with the AKS was a condition of payment. In turn, defendants argued with varying degrees of success that AKS violations did not result in the filing of false claims because compliance with the AKS was not a condition of payment.

5.2 The Eliminating Kickbacks in Recovery Act of 2018

Effective October 24, 2018, the Eliminating Kickbacks in Recovery Act of 2018 (EKRA) created a criminal provision with severe penalties for receiving or paying a kickback (or any remuneration) for referrals to recovery homes, clinical treatment facilities, and clinical laboratories.[8] EKRA does not replace or amend the federal AKS or protect any conduct from prosecution under the AKS, though as noted later it does incorporate the AKS's personal services and management contracts safe harbor. EKRA, unlike the AKS, relates

---

5. Press Release, *supra* note 24.
6. *Id.*
7. Patient Protection and Affordable Care Act, Pub. L. No. 111-148, § 6402(f), 124 Stat. 119, 759 (2010) (codified at Social Security Act § 1128B(g), 42 U.S.C. § 1320a-7b(g)).
8. The Eliminating Kickbacks in Recovery Act of 2018, H.R. 6, 115th Cong. § 8122 (2018), https://www.congress.gov/bill/115-congress/house-bill/6/text#toc-HB10 AD8D0FD9C456F81EE0083634020CB.

to services covered by any "health care benefit program," which is defined to include commercial insurers as well as government health care programs, and thus it greatly expands the scope of potential liability for kickback-related violations.[9]

Specifically, EKRA prohibits, with respect to services covered by a health care benefit program, knowingly and willfully:

> (1) soliciting or receiving any remuneration (including any kickback, bribe, or rebate) directly or indirectly, overtly or covertly, in cash or in kind, in return for referring a patient or patronage to a recovery home, clinical treatment facility, or laboratory; or (2) paying or offering any remuneration (including any kickback, bribe, or rebate) directly or indirectly, overtly or covertly, in cash or in kind—
>> (A) to induce a referral of an individual to a recovery home, clinical treatment facility, or laboratory; or
>> (B) in exchange for an individual using the services of that recovery home, clinical treatment facility, or laboratory.[10]

Violations of EKRA are subject to fines of not more than $200,000, imprisonment of not more than ten years, or both, for each occurrence.

EKRA establishes seven statutory exceptions, five of which thematically mirror existing AKS safe harbors but differ in some respects. Unlike the AKS, EKRA creates an exception for alternative payor models. The statutory exceptions are:

- Discounts or other reductions in price obtained by a provider of services or other entity under a health care benefit program if the reduction in price is properly disclosed and appropriately reflected in the costs, claims, or charges made by the provider or entity;

---

9. "Health care benefit program" is defined as "any public or private plan or contract, affecting commerce, under which any medical benefit, item, or service is provided to any individual, and includes any individual or entity who is providing a medical benefit, item, or service for which payment may be made under the plan or contract." 18 U.S.C. § 24(b).
10. *Id.* at § 220.

- Bona fide employee compensation made to employees or independent contractors, if the payment is not determined by or does not vary by the volume of referrals, tests, procedures, or billings;
- Medicare Part D discounts furnished to beneficiaries;
- Payments made as compensation for services performed under personal services and management contracts that meet the AKS safe harbor;
- Copay waivers made in good faith and not as a matter of routine;
- Transfer of goods, items, services, donations, or loans set out in writing that are medical or clinical in nature and contribute meaningfully to the health center's ability (among other requirements) to serve a medically underserved population; and
- Remuneration made pursuant to an alternative payment model or pursuant to a payment arrangement used by a state, health insurance issuer, or group health plan approved by the U.S. Department of Health and Human Services (HHS).[11]

Another complicating factor is that DOJ, in consultation with HHS, has the authority to propose regulations clarifying the exceptions and enacting additional exceptions, which could lead to further inconsistencies, given that the OIG promulgates the AKS safe harbors.

To date, enforcement actions under EKRA have been limited. The first criminal conviction under the statute occurred in January 2020, when a Kentucky woman was convicted of violating EKRA by receiving $40,000 in kickbacks from the CEO of a toxicology laboratory in return for referring patients for urine tests at the CEO's laboratory.[12]

5.3 The Stark Law

In the late 1980s, Congress became aware of a growing number of potentially abusive financial arrangements between health care

---

11. 18 U.S.C. § 220(b)(1)–(7).
12. Press Release, U.S. Dep't of Justice, Jackson Woman Pleads Guilty to Soliciting Kickbacks, Making False Statements to Law Enforcement Agents, and Tampering with Records (Jan. 10, 2020), https://www.justice.gov/usao-edky/pr/jackson-woman-pleads-guilty-soliciting-kickbacks-making-false-statements-law.

providers and physicians that, while potentially covered by the AKS, were not regularly prosecuted.[13] Because of the lack of enforcement and perceived difficulty for prosecutors to bring such cases, Congress sought a simpler proscription with clear, "bright-line" rules, and enacted the Ethics in Patient Referrals Act, which is referred to informally as the Stark Law, in recognition of the last name of its chief congressional backer, Rep. Fortney (Pete) Stark.[14]

The Stark Law prohibits a physician from referring Medicare or Medicaid patients for "designated health services" (DHS) to an entity with which the physician or a member of the physician's immediate family has a financial relationship, unless the referral meets an exception under the statute. The Stark Law also prohibits an entity from presenting or causing to be presented a claim for a DHS furnished as a result of a prohibited referral.[15]

An entity that collects Medicare payment for DHS performed pursuant to a prohibited referral must refund all collected amounts. Additionally, a violation of the Stark Law may also result in significant penalties, including civil monetary penalties of up to $25,820 per claim if the entity "knows or should know" it violated the statute. The statute also authorizes a penalty of up to $172,137 per circumvention scheme and exclusion from participation in federal health care programs.[16]

Many arrangements in the health care industry setting implicate both the AKS and the Stark Law. For example, payments by a hospital to a physician for medical director services constitute remuneration that could implicate the AKS. Such payments also would create a compensation arrangement under the Stark Law. Even so, the two

---

13. *See generally* Office of the Inspector Gen., U.S. Dep't of Health and Human Servs., OAI 12-88-01410, Financial Arrangements between Physicians and Health Care Businesses (May 1989).

14. *Id.; see also* JONATHAN E. ANDERMAN, MATTHEW R. FISHER & DONALD H. ROMANO (ED.), WHAT IS STARK LAW? (2014).

15. 42 U.S.C. § 1395nn.

16. The civil monetary penalty amounts assessed for the various civil monetary penalty authorities for all agencies within HHS may be adjusted to comply with the Federal Civil Penalties Inflation Adjustment Act of 1990 (Pub. L. No. 101-410, 104 Stat. 890 (codified at 28 U.S.C. § 2461)). These amounts reflect the maximum adjusted penalty as of December 2021. 42 C.F.R. § 102.3.

laws vary in many respects. Perhaps the most important difference is the fact that no wrongful intent or culpable conduct is required for a violation of the Stark Law to occur. The statute's prohibitions are triggered purely by the structure of the relationship between the entity furnishing the DHS and the physician, and a violation occurs unless an exception is met. In contrast, the AKS is a criminal statute that requires proof of criminal intent to induce referrals. Centers for Medicare and Medicaid Services (CMS) also made efforts to decouple the AKS regulations and the Stark Law regulations in its final rule released on December 2, 2020. Previously, many of the exceptions to the Stark Law included a requirement that the arrangement not violate the AKS, which garnered criticism since the requirement introduces intent as an element of Stark Law compliance despite the fact that the Stark Law is a strict liability statute. CMS removed the AKS compliance requirement for most exceptions, though notably not for the fair market value exception.

The major distinctions between the two statutes may be summarized as shown in Table 2.

Table 2. Distinctions between the Anti-Kickback Statute and the Stark Law

Law	Application	Intent Standard	Exceptions/ Safe Harbors	Possible Penalties
Anti-Kickback Statute	Arrangements with anyone; all federal health care program business	Knowingly and willfully (but specific intent not required)	Failure to comply fully with a safe harbor does not necessarily result in a violation.	Criminal statute: Fines Imprisonment Civil penalties Exclusion
Stark Law	Arrangements with physicians (or their immediate family members); only Medicare Part B and (potentially) Medicaid	Strict liability (i.e., no intent required)	Failure to comply with an exception results in a violation.	Civil statute: Refunds/denial of payment Civil penalties Exclusion

5.4 Civil Monetary Penalties Law

The Social Security Act authorizes the Secretary of HHS to seek civil monetary penalties under the Civil Monetary Penalties Law (CMPL).[17] In turn, the Secretary of HHS delegated the authority to impose civil monetary penalties to the Office of Inspector General (OIG) for HHS. Civil monetary penalties may be imposed for a wide variety of misconduct.

The CMPL provides that any person (including an organization, agency, or other entity, except for beneficiaries) who violates the AKS shall be subject, in addition to any other penalties prescribed by law, to a civil monetary penalty of $105,000 for each such act.[18] Violators will also be subject to an assessment for damages of not more than three times the total amount of remuneration at issue, regardless of whether a portion of the remuneration was offered, paid, solicited, or received for a lawful purpose. In addition, the Secretary of HHS may make a determination in the same proceeding to exclude the person from participation in federal health care programs and to direct the appropriate state agency to exclude the person from participation in any state health care program.[19]

5.4.1 Beneficiary Inducement CMPL

The AKS prohibits illegal remuneration in a variety of contexts, including the provision of such inducements to beneficiaries. Historically, prosecutors have been reluctant to bring cases where beneficiaries have received something of value. As a result, Congress enacted the parallel remedy of the Beneficiary Inducement CMPL, which prohibits the offer or payment of remuneration to any Medicare or Medicaid beneficiary, when the person making such a payment knows that the remuneration is likely to influence the beneficiary to order or receive from a particular provider, practitioner, or supplier

---

17. *Id.*
18. 42 U.S.C. § 1320a-7a(a)(5).
19. *Id.*

any item or service for which payment may be made, in whole or in part, under the Medicare or Medicaid programs.[20] Violation of this prohibition can result in a civil monetary penalty of up to $21,113 for each item or service ordered, in addition to any other penalties prescribed by applicable law. In addition, violators are subject to an assessment of up to three times the amount claimed for each item or service and may be subject to exclusion from participation in state and federal health care programs.[21]

The statute defines the term "remuneration" to include (1) the waiver of coinsurance and deductible amounts (or any part thereof), and (2) transfers of items or services for free or for other than fair market value.[22] The OIG has expressed concern that offering gifts to patients to influence their choice of Medicare or Medicaid providers will affect the quality and cost of the care provided. For example, such practices might create an economic incentive for providers to "offset the additional costs attributable to the giveaway by providing unnecessary services or by substituting cheaper or lower quality services."[23] But the OIG issued a policy statement interpreting the Beneficiary Inducement CMPL to permit providers to offer beneficiaries inexpensive services or items (other than cash or cash equivalents) that have a retail value of no more than $15 per item or $75 in the aggregate per patient on an annual basis.[24]

The Beneficiary Inducement CMPL and the applicable regulation also includes a number of limited exceptions as to what constitutes

---

20. 42 U.S.C. § 1320a-7a(i)(6).
21. Office of Inspector Gen., General Policy Statement Regarding Gifts of Nominal Value to Medicare and Medicaid Beneficiaries (Dec. 2016), https://oig.hhs.gov/fraud/docs/alert sandbulletins/OIG-Policy-Statement-Gifts-of-Nominal-Value.pdf.
22. *Id.*
23. *See id.*; 42 C.F.R. § 1003.101. For example, specifically excluded from the definition of "remuneration" is "[t]he waiver of coinsurance and deductible amounts by a person, if the waiver is not offered as part of any advertisement or solicitation; the person does not routinely waive coinsurance or deductible amounts; and the person waives coinsurance and deductible amounts after determining in good faith that the individual is in financial need or failure by the person to collect coinsurance or deductible amounts after making reasonable collection efforts." 42 C.F.R. § 1003.101; see also 79 Fed. Reg. 59,717 (proposing to expand exceptions to definition of remuneration).
24. 42 C.F.R. § 1003.110.

"remuneration."[25] Of note, remuneration that fully satisfies an AKS safe harbor also is protected from liability under the CMPL.[26] But the inverse is not true, and compliance with an exception to the CMPL does not afford protection under the AKS. In addition, following are brief overviews of key exceptions to the Beneficiary Inducement CMPL:

- **Waivers of Coinsurance and Deductible Amounts.** This exception is specifically excluded from the definition of "remuneration" "[t]he waiver of coinsurance and deductible amounts by a person, if the waiver is not offered as part of any advertisement or solicitation; the person does not routinely waive coinsurance or deductible amounts; and the person waives coinsurance and deductible amounts after determining in good faith that the individual is in financial need or failure by the person to collect coinsurance or deductible amounts after making reasonable collection efforts."

- **Retailer Rewards.** This exception permits retailers to offer or transfer coupons, rebates, or other rewards for free or less than fair market value if the items or services are available on equal terms to the general public and are not tied to the provision of other items or services reimbursed in whole or in part by Medicare or Medicaid.[27] Note that this exception only applies to "retailers," which the OIG defines as an entity that primarily sells items directly to consumers, including pharmacies, online retailers, and entities that sell a single category of items.[28]

- **Preventive Care.** This exception permits incentives "given to individuals to promote the delivery of preventive care services where the delivery of such services is not tied (directly or indirectly) to the provision of other services reimbursed in whole or in part by Medicare or an applicable state health care

---

25. *Id.*
26. 81 Fed. Reg. 88368, 88399–88400 (Dec. 7, 2016).
27. 42 C.F.R. § 1003.110.
28. 63 Fed. Reg. 14393, 14395 (Mar. 25, 1998); 81 Fed. Reg. 24400, 24409 (Apr. 26, 2000).

program."[29] The incentives may not be in the form of cash or cash equivalents and may not be disproportionate to the value of the preventive care provided. Examples provided by the OIG of permissible incentives under this exception include (1) transportation to and from preventive care services; (2) car seats, baby formula, and child safety devices provided for participating in prenatal classes; (3) T-shirts, water bottles, and exercise videos provided for participating in a post-cardiac care fitness program; and (4) blood sugar screenings, cholesterol tests, and medic alert jewelry.[30]

- **Promotes Access to Care.** This exception excludes remuneration that "promotes access to care" and "poses a low risk of harm" to patients and federal health care programs.[31] The OIG interprets "promoting access to care" as "improving a particular beneficiary's, or a defined beneficiary population's, ability to obtain items and services payable by Medicare or a State health care program."[32] Remuneration would pose a low risk of harm by (1) being unlikely to interfere with, or skew, clinical decision-making; (2) being unlikely to increase costs to federal health care programs or beneficiaries through overutilization or inappropriate utilization; and (3) not raising patient safety or quality-of-care concerns.[33]
- **Financial Need.** This exception protects the offer or transfer of items or services for free or less than fair market value, provided that the offeror makes a good faith determination that the recipient is in financial need and the items or services are not offered as part of any advertisement or solicitation.[34]

The OIG recently made changes to the applicable regulation, effective December 2, 2020. The changes included a new exception for

---

29. 42 C.F.R. § 1003.110.
30. *Id.*
31. *Id.*
32. *Id.*
33. *Id.*
34. *Id.*

telehealth technologies for in-home dialysis and new safe harbors for local transportation provided to beneficiaries and arrangements for patient engagement and support, which are both potentially applicable to arrangements that could implicate the Beneficiary Inducement CMPL.

5.5 State Kickback Laws

Many states have their own kickback statutes that contain language similar or identical to the federal AKS. Some are limited to payments made to induce Medicaid or other state health program business while others cover all payors, including commercial health insurance plans. In most cases, there is little case law or other guidance regarding application of state kickback laws. Although most are not as broad in scope as the AKS, and some states would be unlikely to prosecute if an arrangement complies with the federal AKS, any arrangements that may violate state kickback laws should nevertheless be carefully analyzed.

Index